OVERTIME

ALSO BY Philip Whalen

OVERTIME

Selected Poems

Philip Whalen

EDITED BY *Michael Rothenberg*
INTRODUCTION BY *Leslie Scalapino*

PENGUIN POETS

PENGUIN BOOKS
Published by the Penguin Group
Penguin Putnam Inc., 375 Hudson Street, New York, New York 10014, U.S.A.
Penguin Books Ltd, 27 Wrights Lane, London W8 5TZ, England
Penguin Books Australia Ltd, Ringwood, Victoria, Australia
Penguin Books Canada Ltd, 10 Alcorn Avenue, Toronto, Ontario, Canada M4V 3B2
Penguin Books (N.Z.) Ltd, 182–190 Wairau Road, Auckland 10, New Zealand

Penguin Books Ltd, Registered Offices:
Harmondsworth, Middlesex, England

First published in Penguin Books 1999

10 9 8 7 6 5 4 3 2

LIBRARY OF CONGRESS CATALOGING IN PUBLICATION DATA
Whalen, Philip.
    Overtime: selected poems / Philip Whalen; edited by Michael
Rothenberg: introduction by Leslie Scalapino.
        p.   cm.—(Penguin poets)
    Includes index.
    ISBN 0 14 05.8918 X
    I. Rothenberg, Michael.   II. Title.
PS3545.H117A6   1999
811¢.54—dc21   98–48926

Printed in the United States of America
Set in Stempel Garamond
Designed by Richard Oriolo

This Work is dedicated to the following: Lloyd Reynolds, my first teacher; Donald M. Allen, Jim Koller, and Bill Brown at Coyote Books; Bill Thomas; and Zentatsu Richard Baker Rōshi for his teaching and encouragement.

CONTENTS

*

INTRODUCTION

*

I N *Overtime: Selected Poems*, editor Michael Rothenberg, working in conversation with Philip Whalen, drawing from all of his books of poetry, has created a remarkable volume, which includes Whalen's major poems written over a period of approximately thirty-eight years. *Overtime* demonstrates Whalen's own clarification of his intention: "This poetry is a picture or graph of a mind moving, which is a world body being here and now which is history . . . and you . . . not ideogram, not poetic beauty" (in the poem "Since You Asked").

Whalen developed his poetics in the company of fellow members of the Beat movement, Allen Ginsberg, Gary Snyder, Michael McClure, Diane di Prima, Jack Kerouac, Joanne Kyger, and alongside other poets such as Robert Duncan, Charles Olson, Robert Creeley, and Jack Spicer.

Akin to Stein, in the writing being nonrepresentational, realistic in that it is phenomenological rather than visionary, Whalen isn't describing a subject; that is, it's not "about" something—rather, the writing *is* the mind's operations per se. It's playfulness, for one thing.

The most formally radical of the Beat poets, Whalen not only posits the poetry to be a graph of the mind moving, but he contrives to break that mind apart: writing is to make no connection as it's being in the instant of and being the act of disjunction.

Philip Whalen's writing is the occurrence of time as being, or being as time; similar to Zen master Dōgen's articulation of "being" as past/present/and future, which are occurring separate and simultaneous: "all times at once."

In Whalen's writing, comparable to Dōgen's teaching (the poetry not being a description of anything outside, but a demonstration of one's mind doing this), the nature of the present is only disjunctive; the times occurring separately are at the same time.

His poetry, apparently conversational, may be a series of non sequiturs. Only the disjunction is there, occurring by the action (of the mind making leaps and remarks, and imitating its own sound and conversation which is to itself or others); but there is the backlog at the same moment that is *range* itself. An implied vast space and terrain—which is history, the outside at present, his memory, dreams as their occurrence or unfolding (not as their having been interpreted after), phrases from books and from conversations overheard.

The syntax and structure of the poetry imitates or duplicates the process of the reader's own mind-phenomena, so that one is reading as going through the process that is one's own mind.

Assertions are at the same time changed by a different simultaneous perspective. The poem is one's always leaping out of one's mind, not being in the same moment of one's mind *there*.

Commenting on his assertion that his poetry is "a world body here and now which is history," Whalen deadpans assertion, removing its ground by humorously asserting, "I do not put down the academy but have assumed its function in my own person, and in the strictest sense of the word—*academy:* a walking grove of trees."

"Olson told us that history was ended." Making fun of himself and Olson, he modestly, humorously mirrors Olson ending history; in that the subject is occasional, transience itself. Boisterous and elegant, grave cumulatively, Whalen's poems are history as disjunction, that being sound-shape. They are their language shape/measure.

He cited *The Art of the Fugue* as a source. A fugue is a composition of melodies, a melody being horizontal movement. His long poems are subtle music structures, compressed shimmering panels in a contemporary American idiom—an element of which is for one to get out of one's head: "I sail out of my head, incandescent meditations." Whalen's poetry, as he says about Thelonious Monk's compositional method, "has the music going on all the time." Referring to Monk: "you see him listening to it when he's out walking around/it's *going* all the time." But Whalen adds, "The best music I make myself . . . Quite seriously the best is my own/Heard in a dream."

He wrote in a notebook making drawings or doodles alongside the poetry, as if the doodling were graphs of or visual extensions alongside the poems, as such part of the writing. Whalen comments within *Scenes of Life at the Capital* that the process of copying from the manuscript to the typewriter suppresses the material. The handwritten text in calligraphy was as much drawing as the doodlings and constituted a layering in the notebooks of "experience" that is physical gesture of the hand in writing. The text transmogrified into type, with the drawings-doodling retained, gives an "impression" of an original past (a first layer), no longer in existence but still "influencing" the text.

One of Philip Whalen's poems might be written over a period of several years in a notebook, then typed and chopped into separate lines which, arranged on the floor, are comparisons of different moments or periods of time and his mind at those times. Thoughts would have similarities and differences in two times. "It is not collage"—Whalen made the distinction speaking to me. Collage would be a completed woven or superimposed fabric (when read later); rather the levels in the writing maintain their first imprint, the pattern of what the mind was doing at those different times. Is the distinction that a collage is more passive as a construction in the sense that the viewer sees it later, rather than active comparison on the part of the reader and writer in reading as real-time, an activity? The way we remember hearing music in a dream, Whalen's writing in the long poems is his mind-structuring at different periods, or the mode of a thought or sensation's occurrence then.

Similar to the composition of a fugue with multiple recurring melodic lines, the long poems are all times at once. In "Life in the City" and *Scenes of Life at the Capital*, all capitals are occurring at once, Kyoto (Lady Murasaki's tenth-century Kyoto, and Kyoto in modern Japan), Rome, London, Venice, Padua; the cities, like his lists of words staggered ("running" concurrently, vertically) beside horizontal passages, are separate realms occurring together at the same time. Those vertical lists of words beside horizontal "passages of events" are not ideograms (Pound's notion derived from Chinese characters in which multiple images are simultaneous as components of one character), but rather the reader's process of apprehending simultaneous action 'as they occur.'

Pound used the ideogram as placement adjacent to each other of references or events. Consecutive passages of text on a page say, which do not have a 'relation' as narrative. Yet Whalen goes further: there *not* being an inherent relation in the content of two phrases, placed beside each other, becomes an action. The poetry then is phenomenal action as if outside the writer's mind even—as being its operations.

Whalen's writing is imitations of his own speaking, imitations of his mind as being 'only' illusions, rather than the writing *dramatizing* conflicting postures (in the sense of posturing, which is to portray his own psychology or conflicts). In other words, he makes constructions overt as voices simultaneously as their being the ego of the speaker. So it displaces it by occurring at the same time ("wrecks the mind").

The voices of the writing do not 'frame' a personality in the sense of making it possible to reconstruct that as a cohesive whole. Whalen's writing of history as only being 'now' deconstructs overviews and assertions: by rendering details as the phenomena of events and rendering interpretation of events as being *also* phenomena.

Similar to his drawings being the 'impression' in the text of the physical gesture of the hand, the imitation of his own internal or conversational voice as mind-phenomena is also an 'impression,' an 'imprint' of spoken, conversational language. As if the illusion of an illusion. The text as spoken language or the structure of a conversation is an activity which can be only at present for (or with) the reader. That is, the reader (in the activity of reading, or listening) responds as to a conversation with someone else.

The poetry is ventriloquism which by being sensitive scrutiny of himself is actual conversation. The 'imprint' of someone only as their speaking has a shape that is the text.

He was writing for the sake of finding something out, the imagination as he said being the only thing that's genuine—writing "for fun/For boredom. For nothing," concertedly and outside of any notion of a field or discipline. He was in fact making a countergesture to the academy.

He was critical of the "academy" in the same way he noted characteristics of America or the transpiring of the Vietnam War—as streams of events occurring or opinions that create events by repression of the actual nature and activity of the events.

Perceiving is the same as the events of the poetry. Reading or listening to Whalen's poetry, one doesn't have to 'figure it out.' The reader isn't spending time figuring out either the process of perception or what is transpiring. One does not usually focus on one's own process of perception while perceiving—Whalen brings us to do that as being in a state of mind, not by viewing from outside; just as one speaking isn't foreseeing a spontaneous conversation.

A characteristic of repression, in reading, is having the assumption that there is a cohesive whole (of social/private/phenomenal reality), which is then the basis of interpretation—that is, which uses the contents or story-element of the poetry, equating that with the poet's personality then seen as entity. Whalen was speaking in the writing of that outside interpretation, which coalesces or reconstructs a world which is its own assumption—that is, reading seeking a cohesive whole whereas the poetry (Whalen's poetry) is indicating this process as illusion and is deconstructing it.

Repression of the real occurs by seeing events and thoughts (all of which are changing) as fixed, as representational of that cohesive reality which that reading itself constantly reconstructs.

Whalen identifies this circular process as the 'constructing' of history, rather than history being the transpiring of events (rather than it being what it is). He's saying that we don't either have to substantiate that 'construction' as bearing it out, or be answerable to it. All times being brought together and separate simultaneously ("wreck the mind") is there being no 'history' *then*.

Addressing William Carlos Williams, he uses the word "LITERATURE" to mean history already constructed rather than poetry which is living community:

LITERATURE
  AMERICAN
    LITERATURE!
they never really let you into that, in spite of
your book that all professors love, In the American Grain
that fills my shoes with sorrow and gets between my teeth

  I want to be a world, not just another
  American tinky poetty-boo

Comparing distinctions which are the layers as states of mind in different times, as if these are the sound/shape that's the writing, is the 'interior' motion of 'experience.'

His gesture, like Williams and Stein, is that the language is only its occurrence. Whalen adds to their accomplishment examining mind-phenomena as shape and sound. 'Wrecking the mind' is *that*—in the disjunct non sequitur as in the transpiring in the long poems of all times together. The poetry is a world itself in continually 'noting' the reconstructing of a cohesive whole (by the social realm and by itself) by proliferating its own fictions and illusions.

While writing is recognized to be entirely fictional, the factual, exterior world "[i]s not the one I'd find outside this door." It is not itself (as we see it) what we think it is. The examples don't demonstrate or illustrate. "I keep hearing something else" (which is the music or pattern going at the same time)—hearing that music is related to or a corollary of phenomena as: "the world's invisible."

Whalen forswore "poetic beauty" and the volume *Overtime* reads as a structure of shifting, shimmering continents or times, which really are incandescent meditations in that the reader is in the pleasure of reading, fully alerted.

—LESLIE SCALAPINO

OVERTIME

The Road-Runner

FOR L. J. REYNOLDS

Thin long bird
     with a taste for snakes' eyes
Frayed tail, wildcat claws
His pinions are bludgeons.

Few brains, topped
By a crown
And a flair for swift in-fighting—
Try to take it from him.

23:iii:50

Homage to Lucretius

It all depends on how fast you're going
Tending towards light, sound
Or the quiet of mere polarity

      Objects: Slowness

Screen
      A walking sieve
Wide-open and nowhere
The mountains themselves
Picked up into turnips, trees
Wander as bones, nails, horns

And we want crystals,
Given a handful of mercury
      (Which can be frozen into a pattern vulnerable to body heat)

The notion intimidates us
We can't easily imagine another world
This one being barely
Visible:
      We lined up and pissed in a snowbank
      A slight thaw would expose
      Three tubes of yellow ice

And so on . . .
A world not entirely new
But realized,
The process clarified
Bless your little pointed head!

1952

"Plus Ça Change . . ."

What are you doing?

    I am coldly calculating.

I didn't ask for a characterization.
Tell me what we're going to do.

    That's what I'm coldly calculating.

You had better say "plotting" or "scheming"
You never could calculate without a machine.

    Then I'm brooding. Presently
    A plot will hatch.

Who are trying to kid?

    Be nice.

    (SILENCE)

Listen. Whatever we do from here on out
Let's for God's sake not look at each other
Keep our eyes shut and the lights turned off—
We won't mind touching if we don't have to see.

    I'll ignore those preposterous feathers.

Say what you please, we brought it all on ourselves
But nobody's going out of his way to look.

    Who'd recognize us now?

We'll just pretend we're used to it.
(Watch out with that goddamned tail!)

Pull the shades down. Turn off the lights.
Shut your eyes.

(SILENCE)

There is no satisfactory explanation.
You can talk until you're blue

    Just how much bluer can I get?

Well, save breath you need to cool

    Will you please shove the cuttlebone a little closer?

All right, until the perfumes of Arabia

    Grow cold. Ah! Sunflower seeds!

Will you listen, please? I'm trying to make
A rational suggestion. Do you mind?

    Certainly not. Just what *shall* we tell the children?

28:ix:53
1:ii:55

If You're So Smart, Why Ain't You Rich?

I need everything else
Anything else
    Desperately
But I have nothing
Shall have nothing
    but this
Immediate, inescapable
    and invaluable
No one can afford
    THIS
Being made here and now

    (Seattle, Washington
      17 May, 1955)

MARIGOLDS

Concise (wooden)
    Orange.
Behind them, the garage door
    Pink
(Paint sold under a fatuous name:
"Old Rose"
    which brings a war to mind)

And the mind slides over the fence again
Orange against pink and green
Uncontrollable!

Returned of its own accord
It can explain nothing
Give no account

What good? What worth?
        Dying!

You have less than a second
        To live
To try to explain:
Say that light
        in particular wave-lengths
        or bundles wobbling at a given speed
Produces the experience
Orange against pink

Better than a sirloin steak?
A screen by Korin?

The effect of this, taken internally
The effect
            of beauty
                        on the mind

There is no equivalent, least of all
These objects
Which ought to manifest
A surface disorientation, pitting
Or striae
Admitting *some* plausible interpretation

But the cost
Can't be expressed in numbers
Dodging between
        a vagrancy rap
        and the newest electrical brain-curette
Eating what the rich are bullied into giving
Or the poor willingly share
Depriving themselves

More expensive than ambergris
     Although the stink
          isn't as loud. (A few

Wise men have said,
     "Produced the same way . . .
     Vomited out by sick whales.")
Valuable for the same qualities
     Staying-power and penetration
I've squandered every crying dime.

Seattle 17–18:v:55

The Slop Barrel:

Slices of the Paideuma for All Sentient Beings

NOTE: "Slices" was suggested as a title by Mike McClure. The anecdote
of the bicycle's demise is the original property of Mr. Grover Grauman
Sales, Jr., of Louisville and San Francisco & used with his kind permission.

I

We must see, we must know
What's the name of that star?
How that ship got inside the bottle
Is it true your father was a swan?
What do you look like without any clothes?

My daddy was a steamboat man
His name was Lohengrin, his ship
The Swan, a stern-wheeler—
Cargoes of oil and wheat between Umatilla
And The Dalles before the dam was built

I want to look at you all over
I want to feel every part of you

So we compare our moles and hair

You have as many scars as my brother, Polydeuces
That's the only mole I've got
Don't look at it. I worry sometimes it will
Turn into cancer. Is that the mark of Asia
On your body? It is different from my husband's.

It was done when I was born
A minor sacrifice to Astarte (the priests
Lose everything)
A barbarous practice, I suppose.

Gods demand a great deal. This coming war
Nothing will be saved; they claim
It will rid the earth of human wickedness . . .

Nevertheless when we are vaporized
To descend as rain across strange countries
That we will never see
The roses will grow human ears for petals
To hear the savoy cabbages philosophize.

I I
You say you're all right
Everything's all right
Am I supposed to be content with that?

    If I told you everything
    You'd have nothing to say
    If I fell to pieces you'd walk away flat
    (A weather-vane)

Suppose we were the first to begin
Living forever. Let's start
Right now.

Do you want this peach?
It's immortal.

    Both my watches are busted.

Meanwhile, back at the ranch
Pao Pu-tzu ("in the latter years
Of a long lifetime")
Is making those pills . . . ("the size of a hemp-seed")

    (I would prefer the hemp, myself
    Since *Sa majesté impériale*

"took a red pill . . . and was not."
None of them artificial kicks for me.)

to show up later
Riding a Bengal tiger
Both man and beast gassed out of their minds
Laughing and scratching
Pockets and saddlebags full of those pills:
"Come on, man, have a jellybean!"

The business of this world
Is to deceive but *it*
Is never deceived. *Maya Desnudata*
And the *Duchess:* the same woman. Admire her.
Nevertheless she is somebody else's
Wife. I don't mean unavailable
I mean preoccupied.

You and me
We make out, the question is
How to avoid future hangups, and/or
Is this one of them now?
We could take a decent time
Figuring out how to avoid repeating
Ourselves

> *I know where I'm going*
> *I been there before*
> *I know when I get there*
> *I'll travel no more*

Do you?
Are you still all right?
I don't want you to freeze.

I guess my troubles are pride
And doubt. You *are*
All right.

Have a jellybean . . .
Here comes a tiger.

I I I
By standing on the rim of the slop barrel
We could look right into the birds' nest.
Thelma, too little, insisted on seeing
We boosted her up
                and over the edge
Head first among the slops in her best Sunday dress
Now let's regret things for a while
That you can't read music
That I never learned Classical languages
That we never grew up, never learned to behave
But devoted ourselves to magic:

    Creature, you are a cow
    Come when I call you and be milked.
    Creature, you are a lion. Be so kind
    As to eat something other than my cow or me.
    Object, you are a tree, to go or stay
    At my bidding . . .

    Or more simply still, tree, you are lumber
    Top-grade Douglas fir
    At so many bucks per thousand board-feet
    A given amount of credit in the bank
    So that beyond a certain number of trees
    Or volume of credit you don't have to know or see
    Nothing

Nevertheless we look
And seeing, love.
From loving we learn
And knowingly choose:
Greasy wisdom is better than clothes.

I mean I love those trees
And the printing that goes on them
A forest of words and music
You do the translations, I can sing.

  I V
Between water and ice
(Fluid and crystal)
A single chance

Helen, Blodeuwedd manufactured
Entirely of flowers
or flames
A trilium for every step
White trifolium, purple-veined
(Later completely purple)

  The heavy folds of your brocade
  Black waves of your hair
  Spilled across the *tatami*
  Black water smashed white at Suma
  "No permanent home"

I just don't understand you, I'm really stumped

Petal from the prune tree
Spins on a spider web
Slung between leaves
A flash in the sun

Baby scrooches around on the rug trying
To pick up the design

  PAY NO ATTENTION TO ME

The pen forms the letters
Their shape is in the muscles
Of my hand and arm

Bells in the air!

At this distance the overtone
Fourth above the fundamental
Carries louder
Distorting the melody just enough
To make it unrecognizable

YOU DON'T LOVE ME LIKE YOU USED TO
YOU DON'T LOVE ME ANY MORE.

The sun has failed entirely
Mountains no longer convince
The technician asks me every morning
"Whattaya know?" and I am
Froze.
Unless I ask I am not alive
Until I find out who is asking
I am only half alive and there is only

WU!

(An ingrown toenail?)

WU!

(A harvest of bats??)

WU!

(A row of pink potted geraniums///???)

smashed flat!!!
The tonga-walla swerved, the cyclist leapt and
The bicycle folded under the wheels before they stopped
The tonga-walla cursing in Bengali while the outraged
Cyclist sullenly repeats:

You *knows* you got to *pay* for the motherfucker
You knows you *got* to pay for the motherfucker

The bells have stopped
Flash in the wind
Dog in the pond.

Berkeley 5:iii:56
11:viii:56

14

Sourdough Mountain Lookout

Tsung Ping (375–443): "Now I am old and infirm. I fear I shall no more be able to roam among the beautiful mountains. Clarifying my mind, I meditate on the mountain trails and wander about only in dreams."
—in The Spirit of the Brush, tr. by Shio Sakanishi, p. 34.

FOR KENNETH REXROTH

I always say I won't go back to the mountains
I am too old and fat there are bugs mean mules
And pancakes every morning of the world

Mr. Edward Wyman (63)
Steams along the trail ahead of us all
Moaning, "My poor old feet ache, my back
Is tired and I've got a stiff prick"
Uprooting alder shoots in the rain

Then I'm alone in a glass house on a ridge
Encircled by chiming mountains
With one sun roaring through the house all day
& the others crashing through the glass all night
Conscious even while sleeping

    Morning fog in the southern gorge
    Gleaming foam restoring the old sea-level
    The lakes in two lights green soap and indigo
    The high cirque-lake black half-open eye

Ptarmigan hunt for bugs in the snow
Bear peers through the wall at noon
Deer crowd up to see the lamp
A mouse nearly drowns in the honey
I see my bootprints mingle with deer-foot
Bear-paw mule-shoe in the dusty path to the privy

Much later I write down:
    "raging. Viking sunrise
    The gorgeous death of summer in the east"
(Influence of a Byronic landscape—
Bent pages exhibiting depravity of style.)

Outside the lookout I lay nude on the granite
Mountain hot September sun but inside my head
Calm dark night with all the other stars

HERACLITUS: "The walking have one common world
But the sleeping turn aside
Each into a world of his own."

I keep telling myself what I really like
Are music, books, certain land and sea-scapes
The way light falls across them, diffusion of
Light through agate, light itself . . . I suppose
I'm still afraid of the dark

        "Remember smart-guy there's something
        Bigger something smarter than you."
        Ireland's fear of unknown holies drives
        My father's voice (a country neither he
        Nor his great-grandfather ever saw)

        A sparkly tomb a plated grave
        A holy thumb beneath a wave

Everything else they hauled across Atlantic
Scattered and lost in the buffalo plains
Among these trees and mountains
From Duns Scotus to this page
A thousand years

        (". . . a dog walking on his hind legs—
        not that he does it well but that he
        does it at all.")

Virtually a blank except for the hypothesis
That there is more to a man
Than the contents of his jock-strap

EMPEDOCLES: "At one time all the limbs
Which are the body's portion are brought together
By Love in blooming life's high season; at another
Severed by cruel Strife, they wander each alone
By the breakers of life's sea."

Fire and pressure from the sun bear down
Bear down centipede shadow of palm-frond
A limestone lithograph—oysters and clams of stone
Half a black rock bomb displaying brilliant crystals
Fire and pressure Love and Strife bear down
Brontosaurus, look away

My sweat runs down the rock

HERACLITUS: "The transformations of fire
are, first of all, sea; and half of the sea
is earth, half whirlwind. . . .
It scatters and it gathers; it advances
and retires."

I move out of a sweaty pool
          (The sea!)
And sit up higher on the rock

Is anything burning?

The sun itself! Dying

Pooping out, exhausted
Having produced brontosaurus, Heraclitus
This rock, me,
To no purpose
I tell you anyway (as a kind of loving) . . .

Flies & other insects come from miles around
To listen
I also address the rock, the heather,
The alpine fir

BUDDHA: "All the constituents of being are
Transitory: Work out your salvation with diligence."

(And everything, as one eminent disciple of that master
Pointed out, has been tediously complex ever since.)

There was a bird
Lived in an egg
And by ingenious chemistry
Wrought molecules of albumen
To beak and eye
Gizzard and craw
Feather and claw

My grandmother said:
"Look at them poor bed-
raggled pigeons!"

And the sign in McAlister Street:

> "IF YOU CAN'T COME IN
> SMILE AS YOU GO BY
> L♡VE
> THE BUTCHER

I destroy myself, the universe (an egg)
And time—to get an answer:
There are a smiler, a sleeper and a dancer

We repeat our conversation in the glittering dark
Floating beside the sleeper.
The child remarks, "You knew it all the time."

I: "I keep forgetting that the smiler is
Sleeping; the sleeper, dancing."

From Sauk Lookout two years before
Some of the view was down the Skagit
To Puget Sound: From above the lower ranges,
Deep in forest—lighthouses on clear nights.

This year's rock is a spur from the main range
Cuts the valley in two and is broken
By the river; Ross Dam repairs the break,
Makes trolley buses run
Through the streets of dim Seattle far away.

I'm surrounded by mountains here
A circle of 108 beads, originally seeds
    of *ficus religiosa*
      Bo-Tree
A circle, continuous, one odd bead
Larger than the rest and bearing
A tassel (hair-tuft) (the man who sat
      under the tree)
In the center of the circle,
A void, an empty figure containing
All that's multiplied;
Each bead a repetition, a world
Of ignorance and sleep.

Today is the day the goose gets cooked
Day of liberation for the crumbling flower
Knobcone pinecone in the flames
Brandy in the sun

Which, as I said, will disappear
Anyway it'll be invisible soon
Exchanging places with stars now in my head
To be growing rice in China through the night.

Magnetic storms across the solar plains
Make Aurora Borealis shimmy bright
Beyond the mountains to the north.

Closing the lookout in the morning
Thick ice on the shutters
Coyote almost whistling on a nearby ridge
The mountain is THERE (between two lakes)
I brought back a piece of its rock
Heavy dark-honey color
With a seam of crystal, some of the quartz
Stained by its matrix
Practically indestructible
A shift from opacity to brilliance
(The Zenbos say, "Lightning-flash & flint-spark")
Like the mountains where it was made

What we see of the world is the mind's
Invention and the mind
Though stained by it, becoming
Rivers, sun, mule-dung, flies—
Can shift instantly
A dirty bird in a square time

Gone
Gone
REALLY göne
Into the cool
O MAMA!

Like they say, "Four times up,
Three times down." I'm still on the mountain.

Sourdough Mountain 15:viii:55
Berkeley 27–28:viii:56

NOTE: The quotes of Empedocles and Heraclitus are from John Burnet's *Early Greek Philosophy*, Meridian Books, New York.

Further Notice

I can't live in this world
And I refuse to kill myself
Or let you kill me

The dill plant lives, the airplane
My alarm clock, this ink
I won't go away

I shall be myself—
Free, a genius, an embarrassment
Like the Indian, the buffalo

Like Yellowstone National Park.

22:ix:56

Soufflé

TAKE I   Carol said, "I looked at all my cells today
Blood & smear samples from all over me.
They were all individuals, all different shapes
Doing whatever they were supposed to
And all seeming so far away, some other world
Being I."

TAKE II   How do you feel?
Me? Oh, I feel all right but sometimes
I feel like a motherless child.
I feel like walking out of here & spending
       vast sums of money. How do you
Feel? I feel with my.

TAKE III   The wind increases as the sun goes down
The weight of that star pulling air after it
Naturally the prune trees blossom now
And some kind of bush with pink trumpet flowers
All the other trees except acacias have quit

TAKE IV   High strato-cumulus clouds and a
Light north-easterly wind (possibly
Two m. p. h. on the Beaufort Scale)
       "What ever became of old Whatch-callum,
       Old what's his name,
       Old . . . you know, the old fellow
       Who had that little ranch out by Mt. Pisgah,
       Out by the Pisgah Home? Had that
       Eight-finger Chinese cook & everything
           tasted like kerosene,
       We went out there once & put up blackberries."

     "Why, Dell, I don't remember . . .
He was a friend of yours."

TAKE V   How do I feel? I'm under it
          Way under but I'm
          Coming out, working out
          The weight, the pressure
          Piles of detritus already removed
          The weight of half the earth, slowly
          You can hear me underneath it all
          Breathing, a faint
          Scraping, a sifting rattle
          Falling away below
          Back towards the hollow center.
          A little more
          And I peer out

TAKE VI   Intolerable
          You don't accept or reject it
          You see it and know.
          There is a difference.
              "You got to wash them dishes
                  (pronounced "deeshes")
              And hesh that clattering tongue!
              Lolly-too dum, too-dum, &c."
          No particular reply because the question
          Isn't a question at all, it's the presence
          Or absence of light
                          among those trees.

TAKE VII Nowhere, this is getting us no-
                          where
          And we need a place to do it.

TAKE VIII I drank myself into a crying jag face down
          On Ginsberg's woolly green rug
          Roaring, "Gone, everything gone,
          Cold, cold, cold, cold, cold!"

          A nearly perfect vacuum at minus 278 degrees
              Absolute
          HORREUR DU VIDE

The Messrs. Ginsberg & Kerouac, also juiced,
Wrapped me in blankets while I froze & squalled

TAKE IX "I want you to go out & amount to something;
I don't want you to be an old ditch-digger all your
               life
Work with your head if you can, let other people
  use their hands"

TAKE X Can you look at a bug without squashing it?
Can you look into a glass without hate, without
Love, without murder?

We have nothing but thoughts of murder, i.e.
Complete ignorance of the world's own nature; or
Where there's no sense there's no feeling.
As for myself, I'm a genuine thug, I believe
  in Kali the Black, the horrific aspect
  the total power of Siva
  absolute destruction
BUT it don't mean
What it looks like
       and the description misleads.

TAKE XI Bud-clusters hang straight down from the sharply-
             crooked
Geranium stem like strawberries, the wild mountain
             kind
These flowers almost as wild right here
Barbarous thick-jointed tangle, waist-high
Escaped once for all from the green-houses of the
             north
A weed, its heavy stalks jointing upwards & winding
             out
In all directions, too heavy to stand straight
The neighbors clipped some out of their yard
The stalks lay in the gutter & grew for days
In the rain water, flowering red
Ignorant of their disconnection

TAKE XII   I shall be in LA
              La Puebla de Nuestra Señora La Reina de los
                                    Angeles
      On Palm Sunday
                    a necklace of skulls & fingers,
                    her belt dangling human arms,
                        legs & heads
                    her several hands brandishing
                        the noose
                        the sword
                        the axe
                        the skull-cup of blood
                        the *dorje* (double lightning-
                                    bolt)
                        Fire
                        Drum
                        Rosary
              Having (DV) arrived by streamline train
                    "Coast Daylight"
           "in a throng of happy apprehensions"

TAKE XIII   Don't you ever get tired
               of your own sunny disposition?

TAKE XIV   I know perfectly well what became of old Mr.
                        Daigler
               Greatly advanced in years he removed from Mt.
                        Pisgah
               To the Odd-Fellows Home in Portland where he
                        died
               Of malnutrition and the radio.

TAKE XV   The whole point of it is,
               When I saw that her necklace was made of my own
               Severed fingers, that I'd only just combed the hair
                    on that skull
                    (now containing lots of my blood
                      & her wasting it, slopping it

All down one of her arms)
She was mine & we made it together
The Island Of Jewels
On a tiger-skin rug

The Sun & Moon shining together.

TAKE XVI   It was so noisy in my head a rush of lights & motion
And music & now the type lies on the page
Perfectly silent, perfectly static, perfect
The same temperature as the space between

Minus 278 ABSOLUTE

radio frequencies in the ten-meter band
from the direction of the constellation
Herakles

Light

Hard radiation (cosmic particles, beta
& gamma rays)

A few vagrant atoms of hydrogen, scat-
terings
of metallic &/or mineral dust shoved along
by the pressure of the

Light

Absolute

o

Berkeley, The Anchor Inn, 23:ii:57
8:iv:57

Literary Life in the Golden West

A Birthday Poem for (&/or about) Mr. J-L. K.,
20:v:57

*

Now we are thirty-five we no longer enjoy red neon
                 (MILNER HOTEL)
We don't know what to do except
Stand on our head four minutes a day
To adjust our metabolism and feel a physical
Ecstasy when we stand up & the blood
Rushes down from our head

It is impossible to write in the big front room
The space, the high ceiling scares us
In the kitchen we write:

> "I have nothing to write about,
> no work to do—I made a pastel picture of the backyard
> I'm reading *Swann's Way*, I talk to my mother & go see
> my friends, they are dull and vaguely busy suffering
> from metabolic disturbances (they don't stand on their
> heads) I just finished writing a book 1000 pages long,
> I'm going away to—or am going to have to manufacture—
> another world, this one is all worn out, Buddha is much
> more interesting than fucking, eating or writing, my
> mother is happy, now I can die next week."

None of our serious friends approve of this
Routine they write articles against us in all
The liberal magazines, the young hitch-hike from New York
And Alabama with their poems, we sit together in Portsmouth
Plaza
Drinking muscatel and swapping stories
Until the buttons drive us home.

10:x:57, 45 Years Since the Fall of the Ch'ing Dynasty

The Summer Palace burnt, the Winter Palace, wherever it was
"Ordre, ordre, Je suis une maniaque pour l'ordre!"
(Meaning that all those sheets are promptly sent to the wooden
Laundries of the Seine,
That all the shoes and sox are lined up in rows
That the words follow each other in ecstatic parentheses, NOT
That you and me are lined up against the innocent wall, torn
By the bullets of righteousness)

I am hid, as William Blake puts it, where nobody can see me not
Even those sad angels who busted the slippery membrane across
My stifled face so I could breathe the incense coming in
From the pavilion under Coal Hill my brocade sleeves raveling
Among the chips of jade and the withered peony blossoms and
The night of the boat-light Dragonboat orgies on the River
In pious memory of whosis that first made the water scene
With an ingenious system of *canali* and Nationally Federated
                                                        Dams
    Where nobody can see me
        I read all about Jimmy Dean with 16 photographs
        and more than a hundred pages of vulgar prose

Nobody can find me I came here with that purpose of being alone
        (R. . . . says we have all these self-destructive impulses and it
        BUGS him, like he went to the neighborhood soda-fountain
        For a coca-cola and everybody/all these monster teen-age
                                                        hoods/
    Jumped on him at once)

Not unlike the United States Marines building teakwood camp-
                                                        fires
Out of the Empress's bedroom furniture on the Phoenix-Viewing
Terrace roasting their wienies.

For My Father

Being a modest man, you wanted
Expected an ordinary child
And here's this large, inscrutable object

      ME

      (Buddha's mother only dreamed
                of a white elephant;
        my mother . . .)

Cross between a TV camera and a rotary press
Busy turning itself into many printed pages
Heavy, a dust-collector, almost impossible
               to get off your hands, out of your house
Whatever it was, not an actual child

You recognize parts of the works, ones you first donated
But what are they doing—the flywheel horizontal
Spinning two directions at once
A walking-beam connected to a gear train turning camshafts—
Which produces material like this
Sometimes worth money to folks in New York
Or not, nobody knows why.

3:i:58

Metaphysical Insomnia Jazz.
Mumonkan xxix.

                                   Of
Course I could go to sleep right here
With all the lights on & the radio going

(April is behind the refrigerator)

      Far from the wicked city
      Far from the virtuous town
      I met my fragile Kitty
      In her greeny silken gown

  fairly near the summit of Nanga Parbat & back again, the wind
      flapping the prayer-flags

"IT IS THE WIND MOVING."
_____

"IT IS THE FLAG MOVING."

Hypnotized by the windshield swipes, Mr. Harold Wood:
    "Back & forth; back & forth."

      We walked beside the moony lake
      Eating dried apricots
      Lemons bananas & bright wedding cake
      & benefits forgot
      _____

"IT IS THE MIND MOVING."
_____

& now I'm in my bed alone
Wide awake as any stone

7:iv:58

20:vii:58, On Which I Renounce the Notion of Social Responsibility

The minute I'm out of town
My friends get sick, go back on the sauce
Engage in unhappy love affairs
They write me letters & I worry

Am I their brains, their better sense?

All of us want something to do.

I am breathing. I am not asleep.

In this context: Fenellosa translated *No* (Japanese word)
    as "accomplishment"

(a pun for the hip?)

Something to do

    "I will drag you there by the hair of your head!"
    & he began doing just that to his beautiful wife
    Until their neighbors (having nothing better to do)
    Broke it up

If nothing else we must submit ourselves
To the charitable impulses of our friends
Give them a crack at being bodhisattvas
    (although their benevolence is a heavy weight on my head
    their good intentions an act of aggression)

Motion of shadows where there's neither light nor eye to see
Mind a revolving door
My head a falling star

7:v–20:vii:58

Hymnus Ad Patrem Sinensis

I praise those ancient Chinamen
Who left me a few words,
Usually a pointless joke or a silly question
A line of poetry drunkenly scrawled on the margin of a quick
                 splashed picture—bug, leaf,
                     caricature of Teacher
         on paper held together now by little more than ink
        & their own strength brushed momentarily over it
Their world & several others since
Gone to hell in a handbasket, they knew it—
Cheered as it whizzed by—
& conked out among the busted spring rain cherryblossom winejars
Happy to have saved us all.

31:viii:58

Complaint: To the Muse

You do understand I've waited long enough
There's nobody else that interests me more than a minute
I've got no more ambition to shop around for poems or love
Come back!
           or at least answer your telephone
I'm nowhere without you

    This is the greatest possible drag
    Slower than the speed of light or always
    A little less than critical mass

    The energy the steam the poop is here
    Everything is (by Nature) Energy, I myself
    A natural thing & certainly massive enough

    A block of lead (the end of all radiation)
    I don't even reflect much daylight, not to speak of
            glowing in the dark
    I'll never get it off the ground

This room is full of 1 fly & an alarmclock
It is uninhabitable

If I wasn't drunk & blowing wine-fumes & peanut breath in your
                          face
Maybe you'd be nice to me.

You do understand
I'd much rather listen, Lady
Than go on babbling this way, O rare gentle
& wise, it isn't enough that your face, your body
Are uniquely beautiful—I must hear you tell me
        about the weather
We might even quarrel if nothing else

You know the answer & don't, won't quit kidding me along
Hanging me up like Sir John Suckling
                in a tag of lace or muslin

I can see right through all those veils
But you can run fast & I've got a bum knee

& you been a long time gone

11–12:ix:58

Prose Take-Out, Portland, 13:ix:58

I shall know better next time than to drink with any but certified
drunks (or drinker) that is to say like J-L. K. who don't fade away
with the first false showing of dawn through the Doug-fir & hem-
lock now here Cornell Road First of Autumn Festival
     a mosquito-hawk awakened by my borrowed kitchen light
     scrabbles at the cupboard door
& the rain (this is Portland) all over the outdoor scene—let it—
I'm all in favor of whatever the nowhere grey overhead sends—
which used (so much, so thoroughly) to bug me
               Let it (Shakespeare) come down
                    (& thanks to Paul Bowles for
reminding me)
there it rains & here—long after rain has stopped—continues from
the sodden branch needles—to rain, equated, identified with no-
where self indulgence drip off the caves onto stone drizzle mist
among fern puddles—so in a manner of speaking (Henry James
tells us)   "There we are."
the booze (except for a hidden inch or so of rosé in the kitchen
jug) gone & the cigarets few—I mean where IS everybody & they
are (indisputably) very sensibly abed & asleep—
         one car slops by fast on overhead Cornell Road the
fireplace pops I wouldn't have anything else just now except the
rest of the wine & what am I trying to prove & of course nothing
but the sounds of water & fire & refusing to surrender to uncon-
sciousness as if that were the END of everything—Goodbye, good-
bye, at last I'm tired of this & leave you wondering why anybody
has bothered to say "The sun is rising" when there's a solar ephem-
eris newly printed, it makes no difference—but you will be less
than nowhere without this pleasurable & instructive guide.

13:ix:58

Self-Portrait Sad, 22:ix:58

At last I realize my true position: hovering face down above the
           world
(At this point the Pacific Coast of The United States)
The lights of the cities & my lives & times there
A second rate well finished nothing too much wrong with it but
           not too interesting
Piece of music—think of De Falla's *Nights in the*
           Gardens of Spain:
Very like that—mildly extravagant, vaguely romantic
Some overtones of a home grown exoticism

Trying to break this all up I meditate a while
Walk on the beach to look at the moon (some sort of festival
           moon surely
First full moon after Autumn Equinox)

Sudden seabird exclamations very loud just over my head invisible

Broken tooth. Shrouded typewriter. Noisy clock. Poorly tuned
           radio.
Sick refrigerator in the next apartment.
I know exactly what I'm doing
& after sleeping and waking again the rest of this day will be
           wonderful

(DREAM PANTOMIME)

Stacked high around us while we practice unspeakable
           vices

Bones of Senacherib his victims
O Babylon, dear Babylon all drowned!

The irresponsible waves & fickle winds
    (Great Atlantis!)

Flying fish & giant cephalopods
Poison floating dumpling Portuguese man o' war
    (O Camoens!)
& immoral Plotinian nautilus high above the temple courts

    Alas dainty Belshazar! Divine Exogamite!
        Perished!

    Folie de grandeur: horror & degradation is my name

Another damned lie, my name is I
Which is a habit of dreaming & carelessness
        no nearer the real truth of any matter
In any direction myself bound & divided by notions

        ACT!   MOVE!   SPEAK!

Forgetting last night's moon & paying no attention now
To the sunlight in these pines

        Deer Demon & Yak Demon stir my brains
        Mouth grows tinier, belly
        Huge—I'm a *preta*, starving ghost
          Self-devoured

PARALYZED AGAIN!

    (*O rage, O désespoire, &c.*)

Swinging in the same eccentric orbit from depression
To mania—imbecility to genius

Unlike Tobit I'm awake but the seagulls mute
        dung as warm as sparrows
            per usual

& I'm tired of being tired of it
A simple switch from hating to loving

That's not enough, walking from one end of a teeter-board
                    to the other
Go sit under a chestnut tree & contemplate the schoolhouse
You won't believe that its thin tall red brick
Peaked roof & elegant cupola with bell
Narrow high green-trim crumble-sill windows (& this
                    is the NEW side, the 1910 Union St. facade
                    the Court St. front is 1897 its great solid doubledoors
                    Sealed)

& now the tree's cut down
                    Oh, well
                    I was never good at throwing rocks to knock down
                    Pods from it anyway, horsechestnuts
                    Cold calsomine smell, solid chunks of brown watered-
                          silk inside
                    To contemplate
                              or decorate with a pocket knife

         DOTE   DOTE   DOTE

Suppose (unbelievably) you were fat & forty for the last 20 years
With sporadic fits of low-frequency radiation
Lots of side-bands, poor modulation, the oscillator
              Unstable

         DOTE   DOTE

(PLEASE REPLACE YOUR OLD TANK WITH A ((PIEZO-
ELECTRIC)) CRYSTAL!   —Yours truly, F.C.C.)

Useless for any practical purpose
i.e. unemployable for clear transmission

    So it was the wrong tree; the school remains
                              &

There's a library not far away
Also brick but under vines with slick blueblack poison berries
A mansard roof thanks to Mr. Carnegie

Mama said: "You don't HAVE to believe EVERYTHING they
        tell you in school—think for yourself a little bit!"

The library: A house of correction
                There is a boardinghouse
                Far far away
                Where they serve hash & beans
                Every Saturday
Intermezzo
                O how those boarders yell
                When they hear that dinnerbell
                O how the boarders yell
                Far far away

Teeter-totter   Contemplate the schoolhouse
Bread & water   Look at the library

        chestnuts

                DOTE

I go home again all the time
It nearly drives me dotty but I go & will go again

                    . . . Far away

& it's as real as anything else
However changed in many particulars—specifically
The love & hate gone out of it leaving what the Friends call
"A concern"
            (is it properly "compassion"?)

                DOTE

I forget how Tobit saw again
    neither school nor library
    not that kind of ignorance
He had to bring some story
Tell the truth on at least one
Occasion or subject
He had to DO
        something first & then the Angels
        The Archangel Raphael, I think?
        brought him eye-cups

Telling you I'm paralyzed—
Inside a thin cast of seagull lime—
None of that was true for more than a minute (vile
                hyperbole!)
You are the ones walking around inside your shells, I soar
Face down high above the shore & sea
        Ho ho, *skreak*, &c.
    Come live on salmon & grow wise!

22:ix–28:ix:58

Something Nice About Myself

Lots of people who no longer love each other
Keep on loving me
& I

I make myself rarely available.

19:xii:58

Take, 25:iii:59

I've run so far in one circle I'm visible now
    only from the chest upwards
Any poet who's really any good
Dances a complicated maze on top of the ground
    scarcely wearing out the grass

A Distraction Fit

I walk around town with my baby
While I'm sound asleep the middle of a nervous breakdown

Big pieces of the world break off
       Slowly
     sleeping
           she didn't know the right way home, I lead the way
                with my eyes closed

Pieces of myself plaster & stucco walls
            Potemkin facades
      drifting away

Lungs breathe me out
Heart circulates me through pipes & tubing
Brains imagine something walking
         asleep

She holds this man by the arm it stretches
         across the world
Hand in his pocket
Dream of love in 2 houses
        asleep
She breathes me in

4:v:59

Haiku for Mike

Bouquet of H U G E
     nasturtium leaves
"HOW can I support myself?"

13:v:59

Address to the Boobus,

with her Hieratic Formulas in Reply

O Great Priestess
O Keeper of the Mystic Shrine
O Holy & Thrice More Holy

Prussian Blue   Dark Blue   Light Blue   French Blue

Blyni & Pirozhki   Sapphire   Aquamarine
To Take Out   Turquoise   Zircon
                        Lapis Lazuli

        Malachite, a sea-color stone

O Hidden!

      (Vestal maenad bacchante)
among the leaves bright & dark

           "... a rubber baby ...
           "... a plastic baby ...
           "cloth baby whose eyes
                close"

O Blessed Damozel
          (flies & lilies)
Rosetti saw you weeping, leaning
    over heaven's gold bar
(Crocodile tears?)
         yellow hair

        "I NEED TO HAVE A PAPER!"
        "... a hand for you, a HAND for you
        a hand!"

Power & clemency
                    VEIL
                              a shroud (only a slip-cover) a curtain
Covering
          from dusty eyes, the vapid gaze of

     THE TABERNACLE & blazing lamps the Molten Sea

& the Sybil also, her eyes closed under the cloth
& covered baskets containing that which none but the initiated
may look upon

                    ". . . I have one
               I have two
               I have a pencil
          I'm going to get another chair
                         & stand up
               I need
               I need to push it
                    THERE!"

                                             10:vii:59

Boobus Hierophante,

Her Incantations

Heavy
Heavy
Hangs

over thy head

"A HAND!
"A HAND!
"A HAND!

This gruesome object was employed in unspeakable rites,
the fingers burning as tapers

WHAT SHALL THE OWNER DO TO REDEEM IT?

TAKE 3 STEPS FORWARD

"A TABLE
"A TABLE
"A WHEEL FOR THE TABLE
"ANOTHER WHEEL FOR THE TABLE
            "RED
            "RED
            "RED
            "RED
            "MONKEY
            "A FLEMING POOL
            "A LITTLE TINY MOUSE RIGHT THERE

full terror

"LOOK AT THAT I MADE!"

10:vii:59

To the Moon

O Moon!
Gradually
      Milo of Croton
Lifting all the seas
    indifferently
Leaf shadows & bright reflections
    simultaneously

13:viii:59

Song for 2 Balalaikas on the Corner of 3rd & Market

We have no peanuts to eat so sad
While looking up tall buildings capitalistic
We cannot return to izba on the steps of Russia Hill
Unless instant money appear in tambourine
             UNFORTUNATELY
The snow is falling in our galoshes
Wolves in our underwear alas poor Czar
Our oatfield crushed under tractors
Varnish falls off our balalaikas all the strings are warped
             we sing out of tune
Give us bread and money, sad,
             SAD!

             *

(With much assistance from Michael McClure, 14:viii:59)

Since You Ask Me

(A Press Release, October 1959)

This poetry is a picture or graph of a mind moving, which is a world body being here and now which is history . . . and you. Or think about the Wilson Cloud-chamber, not ideogram, not poetic beauty: bald-faced didacticism moving as Dr. Johnson commands all poetry should, from the particular to the general. (Not that Johnson was right—nor that I am trying to inherit his mantle as a literary dictator but only the title *Doctor, i.e., teacher*—who is constantly studying). I do not put down the academy but have assumed its function in my own person, and in the strictest sense of the word—*academy:* a walking grove of trees. But I cannot and will not solve any problems or answer any questions.

My life has been spent in the midst of heroic landscapes which
never overwhelmed me and yet I live in a single room in the city—
the room a lens focusing on a sheet of paper. Or the inside
of your head. How do you like your world?

To a Poet

She sings the music
    pulls you down
She's totally irresponsible
    so are your ears (they're supposed to hear)
But why do you care so much
    for music?

31:xii:59

An Irregular Ode

Once I began to write,
Be ruled by Beauty & her wilfullness
& got no further
Choking and wheezing, subject completely to the selfishness
        of my own history

I don't wonder that you doubt my love
My attention wanders even now, squinting at the moon
      bamboo blinds—I should be with you
        we're only blocks apart

The same imaginary beauty splits us up, I keep chasing
      the one who invents the mountains and the stars
I'm a fool supposing she's someone else than you
      are moss & ferns in forest light

13:i:60

Haiku, for Gary Snyder

                    I S
Here's a dragonfly
                    (TOTALLY)
Where it was,

            that place no longer exists.

15:i:60

A Vision of the Bodhisattvas

They pass before me one by one riding on animals
"What are you waiting for," they want to know

Z—, young as he is (& mad into the bargain) tells me
"Some day you'll drop everything & become a *rishi*, you know."

I know
The forest is there, I've lived in it
     more certainly than this town? Irrelevant—

    What am I waiting for?
A change in customs that will take 1000 years to come about?
Who's to make the change but me?

      "Returning again and again," Amida says

Why's that dream so necessary? walking out of whatever house
alone
Nothing but the clothes on my back, money or no
Down the road to the next place the highway leading to the
mountains
From which I absolutely must come back

What business have I to do that?
I know the world and I love it too much and it
Is not the one I'd find outside this door.

31:iii:60

Dream

Wander through expensive party not for me
Open door into formal diningroom I've offended, they are gone
Step out of window & swing on a velvet rope to top of old wall
       dangerous muddy grass flowers
            the top of the arch! (it collapses as my left foot
            reaches solid rock ridge
               nightmare gulf behind below me)

Funeral on a sunny day in Spring, child procession in festival
clothes
Child in open coffin half seen under giant flower wreaths
            passes

Landscape: barren river valley in high plateau-desert crossed by
two bridges, one a Roman aqueduct, partly lost, incomplete,
worked into new bright girder work repeating enormous arches
across miles of wide valley sunset of a day order and peace
far below the aqueduct, two ruined castle palaces

18:v:60

Historical Disquisitions

Hello, hello, what I wanted to tell you was
The world's invisible
You see only yourself, that's not the world
            although you are of it

Are you there

        hello
        why do you have your head in a sack?
        a roony-bomb dream tank?

    Why you got a banana in your ear?

You where?

                Brown eyes they see blue sky

                The world imagines you
                Figure it's a planet

                        You hear?

        an obscure star in the middle

Once you were pleasure-milk and egg

        Were you there

Now you are eggs of milk between your legs

        Are you there

"I am situated somewhere near the rim of a fairly large galaxy
which is one of a group of same & outside of which a considerable

number take their way at incredible speeds & apparently in the
opposite direction . . ."

> You are a wish to squirt pleasantly
> You want a lot of things & they are nice & you imagine
> They are you and therefore you are nice
> You are a wish to be here
> Wishing yourself
>
> >   elsewhere

"Hello. Try to talk some sense even if you
don't think any
It is history
>   (your mistake: "History WAS")
>
> >   now

>   *

History an explanation of why I deserve what I take

>   *

History an explanation of why I get what I deserve

>   *

> (Through more or less clenched teeth):
> "How can you sit there & look at the faces
> you see in Montgomery Street wiped blank
> from selling whatever brains they got faces
> in 3rd Street blank from facing a lathe all day
> & TV all night African tromped-on faces Asiatic
> hunger faces Washington war-masks & smile at me
> about how after all this is a Moral Universe
> gives me the screaming jumping meemies I thought
> you were bright enough had enough work-experience
> yourself to have some faint idea of . . ."

*

hello.

"THE WIND RATTLES THE WINDOW I CAN'T
SLEEP FRIDAY NIGHT IS VERY LARGE IN SAN
FRANCISCO THE LOWER CLASSES GET PAID ON
FRIDAY & GET ON THEIR WAY TO SPEND IT IN
UPPER-MIDDLE-CLASS CLIPJOINTS THEY CLAIM
AREN'T TOURIST TRAPS THE UPPER CLASSES ARE
LUSHED OUT OF THEIR HEADS DOWN IN PEBBLE
BEACH SUCKING EACH OTHER'S & WILL SKIP THE
SHRINKER MONDAY HE'S GAY HIMSELF THE
SILLY SON OF A BITCH AS LONG AS I'M NOT OUT
HUSTLING SAILORS ON MARKET STREET & ONLY
WHEN I'M LUSHED OUT ON MY OWN PREMISES
(FOR WHICH I PAY EXCESSIVELY HIGH TAXES)

I DON'T CARE"

"The middle classes the middle class is mainly from out of
town (that's what I like about San Francisco everybody's either
up or down) they come & look at us they go away puzzled where
they remain,
                outclassed . . .
                            (they will fight the Rooshuns &c.
                they will fight the gooks & wogs & chinks &
                japs & niggers & commies & catholics & wall
                street & any man that tries to tell them
                different . . .)"

"The upper classes don't bother me a bit except
why do they let themselves be buffaloed into
hiring the creepy managers they do? Faceless men to
represent a legal fiction? The upper
well, the . . ."

            "UPPER CLASSES ARE HARMLESSLY IM-
BECILE THE LOWER CLASSES PRETEND NOT TO EX-

IST (& VERY NEARLY CAN'T, OUTSIDE OF JAIL) THE
MIDDLE CLASS MANAGER MERCHANT BANKER PRO-
FESSIONAL PROFESSIONAL THE SOLID (IT'S THE
CHEESE THAT MAKES IT BINDING) CALVINISTFREUD-
IAN DEMOCRACY SWELLS

& BLOSSOMS!"

TERMINAL LUES ACROSS THE SHOULDERS
OF THE WORLD

"The Roman Empire went to hell when the Romans bought them-
selves a goon-squad; bankrupted themselves trying to enforce moral
and sumptuary laws . . ."

History's now

9:vii:60

Dream & Excursus, Arlington Massachusetts

I see Mrs. Garret opening the glass doors of the tomb, doors of
the wood and glass pavilion that's built over the family vault, four
glass lighted passageways—the windows on three sides framed and
can move up and down as in a regular house—mansard roof,
wrought iron ornaments on top and weather-vane. Small wooden
sign to the right of the tall doors:

"QUIETLY AND PEACEFULLY AT HOME
MADELEINE SUMMERFIELD RATHBURN"

like a doll house with gingerbread decorations, small panes of
colored glass surround the window in the center of each door.
Flowers grow in beds on three sides of the building and on each
side of the walk leading to the entrance.

This is probably an early 1870's tomb. Rather eccentric for Cam-
bridge cemetery—or was it a fashion that lasted for several seasons?
A wooden replica of "the old home place" built over the family plot
to protect the expensive marble, granite stones and concrete curb-
ings from the vast Cambridge weather. An investment and a
burden upon the heirs who must spend something each year on
the place . . . paint job, new shingles, mend the walk, etc. Family
quarrel: flowers or shrubbery for the landscaping? and if shrubs,
what kind, and if hardy perennials, would snapdragons be face-
tious in a cemetery?

Cousin Lawrence infuriated everyone by causing the ornamental
ironwork on the roof to be brilliantly gilded. Cousin Maude
assessed each member of the family 17¢ to pay for the immediate
application of black enamel paint to restore the propriety and
hush the scandal. A secret sympathizer of Cousin Lawrence paid
his 17¢, waited until the black paint was thoroughly dry, and
then—in broad daylight—had his chauffeur drive him (Rolls-Royce

1925) to the cemetery, set up a small tent into which he retired to change from street clothes to painters overalls, and with his own hand painted the ironwork a beautiful Kelly green, the chauffeur steadying the ladder and helping wipe the green paint off his person after the job was done, the street clothes restored, the tent removed. He was driven back to town where he sent a telegram in the name of the cemetery corporation complaining to Cousin Maude about the green paint.

14:x:60

For Albert Saijo

Fireweed now—
Burnt mountain day
Sunny crackle silence bracken
Huckleberry silver logs bears
Bees and people busy.

Rainy mountain years
Trees again—
Green gloom fern here
Moss duff sorrel—
Deer sleep.

Tree fire people weed:
Bright and dark this mountain ground.

18:xii:60

Homage to Rodin

I
"THINKER"
      in the classic peristyle
Shows up in old *New Yorker* cartoons, appears in some houses
      as plaster book-ends

A great ANIMAL
      the biggest goon Rodin could find for a model
      or magnified him, I think most Frenchmen are small
      by nature

ANIMAL for sure (we customarily think "man, human, soul"
      confronted with this kind of creature—"I," "We," &c.
      concomitant fantasies of art, politics, religion)

Rodin says: "ANIMAL: WHO SITS DOWN
      which is one difference, apparently doing
      nothing
      TO CALCULATE, CEREBRATE"
      & that's of the first significance:
      Meat thinking and got hands to build you what he
      Means or throttle you if you get in the way, either
            action
      without too many qualms

"HANDS FEET ARMS SHOULDERS LEGS," Rodin says
We're in the habit of thinking "Man: subject for the psychiatrist"

Old stuff, we say, "Oh, Ro-*dan*. . . .
Rilke's employer . . . oh yes, Rodin, but after all—
Archipenko, Arp, Brancusi, Henry Moore—
Sculpture for our time . . ."
      (they appear in Harpo's Bazzooo, modern, chic,
      seriously discussed in *Vogue*—

Epstein and Lipchitz are OUT, the heroic
tedious as Rodin)

NOBODY KNOWS WHAT IT IS, HULKING BEEFY
NUDE
We all the time wearing clothes and arguing "quest for values"
Forget what we are, over-busy with "who"
The only time we sit still is on the toilet and then
Most of us read, the only quiet and private room
Where we have bodies we wish away

Rodin: "BODY: with head containing brains,
            hands to grab with, build (possibly, the physiologist says
            hands helped enlarge the brain) feet
            to come and go, buttocks for sitting down to figure it
                                                out . . ."

How isn't
It wonderful how
Is it "base materialism" why
Do we insist "There is nothing we can do"?

   I I
LANDSEND: "THE SHADES"

I won't go to the park today informal prospects groups of noble
                                                trees

Playland At The Beach instead
You never saw a merry go round so fast

2 fat old men watch it from a bench
One sings words to the tune everyone else forgot

No amout of sympathetic observation will do any good
Why not get older, fatter, poorer
Fall apart in creaky amusement park and let the world holler

Softly shining pewter ocean
Or let it quit, who cares?

The road to the Palace of the Legion of Honor still broke
About 1000 feet of it don't exist as I walk along the edge
Above the foghorns & dim fishboat passing the rocks
Anise and mustard, pinetrees and fog

Formal building pillared propylon and stoa
        HONNEUR ET PATRIE
Apse and dome and Greek pantheon life-size
A few golfers look at them
Just beyond the apse, Ft. Miley steel fence
Empty concrete bunkers, coast artillery no defense
No more meaning than the gods, a wonder of expenditure
The whole outfit stone marble pipe organ and all built
By a single family, given away (more or less)
Nobody home but Cézanne
Amusement (high-class) park to remember dead soldiers
and the late M. Rodin

No amount of reflection on the noble prospectless dead
No amount of indignation does any good
They are blanked, puzzled-looking (*The Shades*)
They stand heads bent down, three arms pointing towards
The ground that covers them, young burly ghosts wondering

We like to kill each other
We like to grab with both hands with our teeth and toenails
Unless you got sharp teeth and toenails you end up
Watching the merry go round not even a dime for popcorn
Nor anything to chew it

"EVERYTHING WAS ALL RIGHT UNTIL THAT MAN
CAME ALONG & WE DECIDED TO BE KIND TO
EVERYBODY THAT'S THE TROUBLE WITH US NOW
WE'RE TOO KIND WE OUGHT TO KICK THEM ALL

RIGHT IN THE ASS & STAY HOME & MIND OUR OWN
BUSINESS . . ."

which is being mean as hell

Fat kid wants expensive camera Daddy to put two-bits into Cliff
House binoculars his father screams in reply, furious, insane,
"Whaddaya wanna looka them rocks whaddaya gonna see in this
fog?" "Come on!" the fat kid hollers, "Gimme twenny-five cents,
put the twenny-fi' cents in, gimme ten-ficens I wanna see them
!R O C K S! out there is COME ON! Gimme twenty-five cents!"
and his father screaming back at him like he might tear the kid
limb from limb but actually looking in another direction, quite
relaxed

There's all this loose hatefulness rolling around
We spend all our time hating the world, the Russians, the Gov-
ernment the job the noise the cops our friends our families
& ourselves for not changing, rearranging
Not being able to find what to change
Or what we'd use to do the job

A woman plays in the surf
Tight jersey pants, a kind of sweater top with sleeves
Fully dressed but the water doesn't hurt her clothes
Oblivious to her girlfriend hollering at her from the sand
                              at the foot of the stairs
She plunges, laughing, through a wave

   I I I
WATERLILIES (and *Iris*)

Fog washing past Mt Sutro Parnassus the Medical School a mirage
       that city in the sea
Leaves over the sky where these waterlilies grow up
       through my mind
Flowers in the water not to be reached or touched

POOL OF ENCHANTMENT, pink granite curbing says, before
                                        De Young Museum
Short reeds & shrubby island Hiawatha boy blows flute
At cougar pair, one crouching, one setting, their ears
Laid back, enchanted
Black water thick mud at the bottom
Lily bulbs, heads in the dark
Pattern of stars inside, buried lights

First a few lobed circles on the water
Then leaf mountain with pink pecker buds
Open flowers (unmistakably women) that never fade nor wither
Impregnated they withdraw beneath the waves

No mystery, genes in every cell manifest
                themselves
Bulb of the earth showing itself here
                as lilies
The summer flowers, underwater globes of winter
                all the same

                            *

Since you'd gone I hadn't thought of other women, only you
Alive inside my head the rest of me
                ghosted up and down the town alone
Thinking how we were together
You bright as I am dark, hidden

Inside the Museum I see Rodin's *Iris*
Torso of a woman, some sort of dancer's exercise
Left foot down, toes grasping the ground
Right hand clutches right instep
Right elbow dislocating
Reveals the flower entirely open, purely itself
Unconscious (all concentration's on the pose;
        she has no head)

Its light blasts all my foggy notions
Snaps me back into the general flesh, an order
Greater than my personal gloom
Frees me, I let you go at last
I can reach and touch again, summer flesh & winter bronze
Opposite seasons of a single earth.

13:vi:60
1:iii:61

The Daydream

A call from, a pull in some direction (EXCELSIOR!) echoes of the future I will presently look back upon (whether with pleasure or chagrin there is no adumbration—the noise is an excitement of some kind) I must seize upon the present moment, the controls—wheels, levers, pushbuttons, dials—and arrange them in such an order that the future event will bring me something valuable, pleasing, rare. With great annoyance, I realize that I'm further than ever from the wheelhouse, the control-board. How shall I ever reach it in time to prevent the boiler explosion, the collision with icebergs and hay-wagons, then skip immediately to the spotlighted stage to receive the medal, the honorary degree, the hundred million dollar prize?

27:vi:61

That One

He spends lots of time in that all-night movie, a red bandanna handkerchief over the lens of his flashlight so he can read without disturbing the other patrons. As long as it's dark, he sees trolley cars and buses with flames billowing out of all the windows while crowds of people and animals inside burn and scream.

In the daylight the streetcars are quiet, being full of water like aquarium tanks; the drowned bodies inside sway gently back and forth to the motion of the cars.

He reads volume after volume of Stendhal, referring only occasionally to a pocket-sized French dictionary. He pauses rarely to look blankly at the movie screen at the rush of cowboys and Indians, Bette Davis as *Jezebel*. Although it is several miles from his apartment to the theater, he invariably walks to it. He never told anyone what happened, what he saw, the one time he took a taxi downtown; he never rode in one again, nor could anyone persuade him to do so.

10:vii:61

Vector Analysis

What I want? green
       grass under leaf tree and vine
Sunshine all around
           dark and
           muddy ground
    wants I
       air
         no boundaries
  put a hole in your skull bone
        open up the sky
  an equal
        vacancy

that is, a partition, with a hole in it, such as might be installed
in an empty cigarbox. Partitioned, the space in the box has two
parts—as long as the lid is open—but shut the lid and where's
your eyes?

    mallow in marshy ground, the water
    hyacinth is found, caltrop
       sliced with dinner meat
          I
          ?

21:viii:61

71

One of My Favorite Songs Is Stormy Weather

silk
lumber
sawdust
wood
pulp
pitch
turpentine
rayon
paper
syrup
rubber
kapok
chewing gum
frankincense   Acorn   Allspice   lime-flower tea
myrrh   Almond   clove   jasmine
fruit   Avocado   nutmeg   gum arabic
 &   Apricot
nut   Apple lime lichee mace gutta-percha
       Bay   mango loquat coffee oil of eucalyptus
       Beech pear cheramoya pepper amber
       Chestnut peach coconut quinine palm wine
       Crab plum cabbage-heart cascara
       Cherry pomegranate pawpaw birch beer
       Chinkapin prune papaya root beer
       date persimmon breadfruit sassafras tea
       fig   quince   guava
       filbert tangerine olive
       haw   walnut
       hazel mulberry
       kumquat grapefruit
       lemon
       medlar
       nectarine
       orange

I said to myself,
"Why are you angry, why
Are you afraid, try
to like something, look
at that flowering weed or bushlet
that bug, that dirt, and select
choose one and like it: love."

As I walked further I grew happier
and less nervous; although I am an
atheist I pray all the time.

I walk on hills of jewels & gold
   A foolish, wicked man.

20:ix:61

Friendship Greetings

Carelessly all fixed up a can of beer
several cigarets a cup of coffee I don't care
whether school keeps or not
thinking of Frank O'Hara in Paris right this minute
or the basement of the Museum of Modern Art as the case may be.

23:ix:61

Early Autumn in Upper Noe Valley

Bang dang ang S. Philip Martyr Angelus 6 P.M. or

VESPERS

but all that's Huguenot propaganda

VEXILLA REGIS
PRODEUNT

that's the *real*
old time down home hogmaw and chitterlings

FUNK

Mr Wagnall hasn't got a look-in

POSITIVELY NO
POSITIVELY NO

this means you!

"I think *Moon Mullins* is terribly vulgar."
"I stand corrected."
7 October 1961
8 October (Sunday,
or, less specifically)   (Tomorrow) is Krishna's Birthday
San Francisco
"a real sweet little guy"
San Francisco 7 October 1961
Saturday at evening

S. Francis (of Assisi)
S. Francis Xavier
S. Francis de Sales

Why not.   OK

a vote for
Good Taste

7:x:61

The Chariot

FOR JESS COLLINS

I stand at the front of the chariot
The horses run insane, there are no reins
The curtains behind me don't flutter or flap

I don't look worried. Is the chariot headed
               for the edge of a cliff?

Behind the curtains a party's going on
           laughing and talking and singing

I prefer to stand here, my arms folded
           Ben Hur
Or one hand leaning lightly on the guard rail

Watch the horses galloping

Mother and father behind the curtains
           they argue, naturally
             "Who's driving, anyway?"

Wind whistles through my spiky crown
Some hero, some king!

30:iii:62

Song to Begin *Rohatsu*

Overcome with frustration I sing a few songs
Ring a few bells & wish for better times.
A dim and moisture afternoon.

     FIXED? The race
  is absolutely honest. Very
            straight; OEDIPUS UN-
BOUND.
      the same fate, no matter what his
position relative to an imaginary horizontal plane
        D A R U M A
    was there any change.

30:xi:62

Spring Musick

Rain straight up and down upon the sword ferns
      the red camellia flowers
Garden stairs waterfall walkways
        Bach!

      a realization of six partitas
      and a skinflute duet (*nombre soixante-neuf,*
         a figured bass)
Just feel your way along at the beginning
And fake the rest

9:ii:63

For Brother Antoninus

Do these leaves know as much as I? They must
Know that and more—or less. We
See each other through the glass. We bless each other
Desk and tree, a fallen world of holiness.

Blessed Francis taught the birds
All the animals understood. Who will
Pray for us who are less than stone or wood?

28:iii:63

Life and Death and a Letter to My Mother Beyond Them Both

O Muse, get me high out of my mind
       open my head I want   MORT
         COLORS   AUX
music and   VACHES
           blast!
              YES.

an attack of middle age and sobriety
break out of this, recover
      soon as

Right now.   plush.
         outbreak of stupid
           a conspiracy

SILENCE   I ought to be quiet while I'm
               having myself totally chopped?

It moves from right to left.

on Saturday only!
a condition I refuse to accept
a performance I cannot condone
      some sort of complicated
      operating but very
      delapidated lashup

       OUTSIDE?
                          PLUSH.
          ?
                          PLUSH
PLUSH.   INSIDE?

why don't you watch where you're
going instead of tripping over your
own feet clumsy booby

plush.   INSIDE?   there.

ain't any feet in here. How
can I instruct them if I can't
communicate with them, if I
am so far away that they do not
(for all practical purposes) enjoy an independent
                                        existence

a challenge of bright light
        obstinate silence
                    I no longer answer the telephone.
Big dipper straight outside the front door.

                        *

bilge. the wind bothers among the avocado leaves
        pester the glass writing scratching twig WINDOW
                also rattles for airplanes
                        blah. blurt.

                        *

I wish I could remember the song which begins,
        "If I had a talking picture of you."

                        *

I shall revise it completely. I shall render everything into
language of a blinding clarity. It will be so charming and
persuasive to every reader that the entire civilized world
will say, "Surely Jonathan Swift has come again!"

. . . passion, it must create whatever new
and exciting. Permanently. Forever young, completely mine,
but it will seem entirely and exclusively yours. It must
possess a molecular structure similar to heroin. I want the
stuff to be absolutely addicting after the customer has had
a single sniff.

*

?   fakery   ?
?

*

IMAGINE MY CONSTERNATION
Horror & Chagrin . . . !

blooie.   (this means, that there was a break
somewhere on the inside, such as one of the
coolant tubes in a reactor power plant, the
filament in a vacuum tube or electric lamp,
or somebody's (for example) gall bladder,
kidney, spleen, etc.)

I WAS JUST ABOUT

. . . actually a spleen in the

MORTIFIED TO DEATH

moment of its final despair & goodbye
says something more on the order of
B L O O R G L E. . . .

BLESS YOUR HEART, HONEY!

". . . one of these days I'm going to sort through all
that stuff and throw nine-tenths of it all away. I don't know what
I keep it for; no good to anybody, a lot of junk and old keepsakes

that don't mean anything to anybody any more, but a person does kind of hate to throw things like T H I S away . . . ,"

*

> *"Bid self-righteousness be still*
> *Wound the callous breast."*

"CAME TO GRIEF
about it, just over an old diningroom

"When the day   table. There's trouble enough in this
Grows dark & cold   world without fighting among ourselves.
Tear or triumph   We must try to live harmoniously."
harm. . . ."

"LEAD THY LAMBKINS TO THE FOLD
TAKE THEM IN THINE ARMS!"

*

14 May 1963   San Francisco

Dear Mama,

Twenty or thirty years too late here I am writing this letter to you, graveyard or no graveyard, no matter whether we abandoned each other in death, that part's all over with. I know that you are well because a part of your attention is occupied with writing this. No need to wonder how or where or whether you are.

I try to be patient and forgiving and understanding but I'm a flop at it. You told me that there are worthwhile people every-where, in every walk of life, people I can respect, people I must love. I don't know how to explain to you exactly, but I'm afraid it's a matter of my being too selfish and small minded and pre-occupied with my own tiny life—I can scarcely see them, and of course I don't really, most of the time, WANT to see them, I have got myself that far under . . . it's I who need out of the Salem graveyard, not you who were never there anyhow.

I don't think it matters what we name it, you make it on the ideas of God, peace, quiet, organ music and Mrs. Eddy's representations of the character and philosophy of Jesus. It saved you dozens of times hand-running, whether you needed it or not. I don't mean any disrespect, but it seems unnecessarily complicated to me—that system, those names—it worked for you or you worked it—like Yeats and his bent gyres and cones and pulleys and belts and geary numbers—and arrived, like him, beyond this fake life and spooky death. I get the general idea, I have a different set of names, I know it isn't really a problem, that I'm not really beset, either with sin or salvation, goldfish or onion-rolls. But for the past couple of weeks the whole business has been coming up cardboard, fake Easter nests of shredded green wax-paper.

There was this man at the Zoo yesterday, combing through the camel wool with both hands, two ladies kept hold of a rope around the camel's neck and tickled it under the chin while the man hooked the fingers of both hands into the (I presume) shedding wool on the camel's side below the humps and pulled great sheets of wool away, like peeling a sunburn—I expected, judging from how hard the man yanked and tore at the wool, that the camel would scream or at least spit on everybody in sight. Instead, it stood there, looking only mildly annoyed, while the man took its fur and shoved it in a gunny-sack. The man wore a neat grey felt hat, an expensive-looking suit and shoes, a white shirt, necktie, and, if I remember right, a vest. The ladies were very fashionably dressed.

Confronted with prodigies of this kind—or, as I recall, on the day you found me blowing bubbles of molten glass—you'd say, "God is love!" Also if my sister fell down the stairs or if you happened to see an automobile accident, it was the thing to say. I guess it doesn't matter so much what it all means, the thing is more like how do I treat other people, how do I use myself?

This is all so abstract and dim. You were able to make it iron all our clothing, cook our meals, provide us with total security and love. I must be a mouldy old ghost . . . but that isn't interesting, either, I know better.

I forget how or where this began—I wanted to talk to you, I

wanted to speak with you, sensible as you are, and how dear, and
properly remote, I'm not that confused, in time and distance, and
I believe still forgiving after all, and still believing that you know
and feel, I hope you can laugh also, because it's a delight to you,
as well as gentle music, Boston voices, quiet lights—joy and
freedom where you live.

So here we are—I didn't want to take a walk or read somebody
else's book. I've waited most of the day for these words to arrive
at last. Now I can let it go—this paper, this pen, the bad light,
the nasturtiums curling their stems in my table jar, the tea is cold.

All my love,

P.

14:v:63

Plums, Metaphysics, an Investigation, a Visit, and a Short Funeral Ode

IN MEMORY OF WILLIAM CARLOS WILLIAMS

O Muse!
I don't dare summon you
All I ask is that I might come to you
Only to see you, only to look
        at your face
If you're too mad or too busy for a talk
        I'll go home soon.

*

Smog this morning
Hot soupy sun
The mailman brought all the wrong letters
The air stinks, the birds are in somebody else's yard
Boys left a yellow broom in the plum tree
        (the plums are still green, however fat)
I hear the Scavengers' Protective Association complaining
        about the garbage cans, I

        worry about the fragility of my verses
        their failure to sound fresh and new

By God, here's the garbage men stealing green plums!

*

Neighborhood boys must go after them
Free food! How can a tree
                (who is an individual)
Belong to a man? It can't
        be stealing

The tree has manufactured these not quite yet
        sweet sticky plums

        my mouth is full of plastic teeth
        most adults are smokers—we
        have no idea about the taste of plums
            except perhaps a memory
            climbing a tree

St. Augustine had the shame of it all his life
        he says
I think of him, seeing these kids up the tree
        their silly yellow broom too short
        the tree's old and brittle, unsafe to climb

The pears (in his case) being hard as well as
        green, to say nothing of the sin
        which he never worked out
        a soulful bellyache his whole epis-
            copal saintly eternity
        (no death, no dying for him, alas)

The pears of Africa pursue him past the heavenly gates

                *

I can still hear something rattling in my head
Perhaps only the little rocks that keep it pointed
Towards the sky—otoliths, ear-stones

                *

which is (now) the wind, although I see fog
        and smoke linger over the Bay
            3 loader cranes on a ship
                gantries in the fog
        flashcar freeway ramp more stinking smoke

Which was my ears rattling an approaching poet,
Ronald Loewinsohn with news from out of town
            considering the study of English
               a long trip to the Northwest with his wife and son
                  for August

I envy them, I've been thinking of going "home," I still
Think of it although it has nothing to do with me
Wants nothing from me—
To Oregon, all this spring

Hard as it is—I'm hungry, in debt, I own one penny
                  copper money USA
I am still alive, I dance alone in this borrowed room
            I sing to myself
               "Green plums, you won't be ready for weeks
               But I'm fat and purple, full of sweet delight,
               Hidden among bright gold leaves,

               . . . .

It is her wish that I be so

               a wasp bounces up and down one of the
               closed windows—two other windows are
               open, he must
                  take care of himself, I say—
               but I worry for him just the same

Goofy june-bug forgotten poet morning stomp.

and the plums, the voices—the presence of Loewinsohn—
all these brought you in, Williams, quite naturally
making my head rattle, your gentle spirit—goofier
            than you've shown yourself to us in the past
               really goofier than I ever gave you credit for being

I mean the insane poetickal rage that you tried
to channel, to subdue

(notions I hate—rather the fury
and the madness, than the bland
"control" of Messrs. X, Y, & Z who must
((of course)) believe they're also
"in control" of

LITERATURE
AMERICAN
                LITERATURE!)

they never really let you into that, in spite of
your book that all professors love, *In the American Grain*
that fills my shoes with sorrow and gets between my teeth

     I want to be a world, not just another
     American tinky poetty-boo

             I am a universe
        etc.

well anyway

I never knew you well enough to call you "Bill"
And you were either my father or not
And I did say a couple days ago that I sometimes
Think of you as a little no-talent middle-class croaker

You did know the madness of love and sorrow
Why should I have wished on you—oh, the crash of cymbals
Rending of live flesh, glare of torches
Total battiness—frenzy—typewriter out the window
          into Cowley's plum tree "How explain about
          the broke window and chair to the cranky
          landlady Hart Crane go away you are too much
          and we don't really believe you write so good
          as all that"

Your head fell apart gently, piece-meal,
        a slowly oozy ripening cheese

WREATH OF SONG

(*Liederkranz,*   an American invention)

It was painful to watch—even eight years ago when I last saw you
not quite articulate, and your hands terribly crimped, yet
delivering yourself, your love,
                to us

      (I got the window open just this minute
      & prodded the wasp out into the wind)

and you said yes you remembered me

Now I remember you, naturally, Dead or Alive, as the notices
              used to say
And you are wanted—not necessarily New Jersey USA
Here with us wherever plums and poets talk together.

17:vi:63

Three Mornings

1.

Fog dark morning I wait here
Half awake, shall I go back to bed
Somebody next door whistles the *St. Anthony Chorale*
I think of Brahms, a breakfast of chocolate whipcream
               sweet bright pastry
          bits of sugar-blossom in his beard

2.

I wait for breakfast to drop from the sky
foghorns,   cluster of churchbells
                 pale sun butter
           traffic airplane marmalade
salt & pepper avocado branch squeak on window
            I drink last night's cold tea

3.

Clear bluey-yellow sky—a morning here—
grey cloudbank with lights of Oakland underneath
Baywater blacky blue   boatlights
Robin: clink   clink   clink   clank   clink
       (6 *Adhyoya, Brihadaranyaka Upanishad.*)

8:v:63
15:vii:63

Raging Desire &c.

Meat I ate   M E A T   I ate meat

"I want to have a banquet, a real banquet, I'd rather spend
the money on a white tablecloth and great conversation than
fancy food, some roast chickens and white bread but what I
really want is a white tablecloth, a spiritual banquet . . ."
   that was Michael on the telephone

27:ix:63

The Fourth of October, 1963

A cold hand among the clouds.

Inside Stuff

Swede-bread honey and tea to breakfast half a canteloupe
Honey inspires prophecy & beneficent wishes, thus:
    Boundless ancient delight for Frank O'Hara
    Kerouac will get the Pulitzer Prize *Visions of Gerard*
    I shall travel to my death in a far country

    Frank has Hart Crane's eyes.

15:x:63

Native Speech

1.

It's all put away now. I don't want to drag it out again,
have to go to work and move all them things—you do it
some other time. I'll show you some other time, not now.

2.

I had it all smoothed over and then he has to come horning in,
Mr. Big has to go to work and get things all galmed up again,
raise a big stink just because he has to be in on everything.

3.

Well that's a fine how de do. Now I've got to take and hunt up
another one of them things to go on there! One of them little—
well, I certainly am put out!

14/19:x–xii:63

Composition

I tetter I dangle I jingle
Fidget with my fingers ears and nose

Make little repairs—tape or glue
And the floor is filthy again

      putting on hats in front of a mirror
            down in front
            down in back
            slaunchways
                      mugging and posing, thinking of
those beggars Buñuel shows in *Viridiana,*
gesture of one finger, two eyes,
the smallest imaginable shimmy
creates a gigantic bacchanal

Iron straps won't hold it all together
It's already there, a piano—in tune with itself—
        a closed system:
Even if you play on it with feathers, rocks, rubber tubing,
        Dear John Cage

26:iii:64

The Lotus Sutra, Naturalized

I got drunk your house
You put that diamond my shirt pocket
How am I supposed to know?
Laying there in drunk tank
       strange town don't nobody know
Get out of jail at last you say
"You already spend that diamond?"
How am I going to know?

27:iii:64

Early Spring

The dog writes on the window
        with his nose

30:iii:64

The Metaphysical Town Hall and Bookshop

"I was sitting there.   I knew it was her.
I knew she had a message and the message was love."

17:iv:64

The Ode to Music

FOR MORTON SUBOTNICK

Where'd all the music
                    go?
"There's a piano in there, but nobody here can play on it.
Old Clodfelter can sing better than he ever lets on."

                              *

We wait
            for the fire from heaven
            for the maturation of our annuities
            for the new life, new earth
                        (Who's going to pay for the roof?)

                              *

"Georgette used to play just beautiful on her saxophone"
            "Waiting for the *Robert E. Lee*"

                              *

"We got this radio, the cabinet is just gorgeous
I've always loved the way it looks, it's got
                        beautiful wood in it
We listen to *Amos & Andy* and *The Richfield
Reporter*
But I'm asleep by the time *Amos & Andy*'s half over

                              *

I never could stand all that symphony music
All that high tone shrill screechy singing I just hate it
Some of it is beautiful, I guess, but oh God, when they get
Some woman with one of those high shrill sopranos . . .
I just never cared for it at all

*

... but I love nice quiet organ music
it's so soothing and restful I could listen to it for hours
or a violin with it—love to go to sleep listening to it
an organ and a violin

*

Dad and them get a big kick out of playing their fiddles
I never could read a note. Your own Dad has a beautiful voice
I never get tired of listening to him sing."

*

"It's a pleasure if your own kids are doing it,
terribly expensive and you've got to keep after them to practice
—I'm so grateful to my mother, she made me
absolutely made me practice and I'm so thankful for that
today;
        I take such pleasure in my music."

*

The length of a song, a short one by Stephen Foster
Or a hymn, that's all we got time for;
In the middle of a second or third verse,
A whispered conversation is likely to begin, something
We've just recollected (did the music remind us?)
To add to what we were saying
                        before the music began
"... that old Mrs. R. turned around,
gave us a dirty look,
            "SH*H*H*H!"
I don't know who that old cat thinks she is—
            Mrs. Astor's plush horse?"

*

How—or why
            do I fizz and throb
I guess I understand
        Camptown Races, the *Archduke* Trio,
            The Pearl Fishers
(Even if I don't like the first or the last)
are matters of life and death

I congratulate myself
I know all about art and I know what I like
        (Q.: ". . . but you *are* queer, aren't you?"
        (A.: "Yes—
            but I don't
            like
            you.")
What do I know or care about life and death
My concern is to arrange immediate BREAKTHROUGH
Into this heaven where we live
            as music

                        *

the fingers that hear it as it happens
as it is being made, Thelonious Monk
"has the music going on all the time," AG told me
"You hear it while he's at the piano,
you see him listening to it when he's out walking around
it's *going* all the time."

                        *

The best music I make myself, with a piano, or borrow
            a pipe organ
(People think the elephant bells beside my door
are purely decorative:
                    wait until you hear my concerto)
Quite seriously the best is my own
Heard in a dream, I conduct a total orchestra

(from the podium or from the organ console)
A gigantic auditorium (is there an audience?)
I wonder if all that
                              can be heard by other beings—
people from other stars or maybe sea-beasts,
                              just beyond our shore
While I sleep in stillness

                              *

ALIVE! Joyful or horrendous Being,
A goddess, they said,
Or a god,
Meaning that it zooms us away,
We find ourselves dancing,
Singing,
We are changed, we—   who so seriously commanded
So solemnly understood ourselves
the world,

Spin,
Leap and holler,
Out of our skulls
Life and death no problem, not interesting,
Free in the air as in happiest vision dream

                    A W A K E !

and smiling (weeping)
We dance
                    together and apart
Awake and tireless
We soar beyond clouds and lights are music
Which streams from our moving
body mind laugh leap

                                        2:iii:64
                                        2:v:64

102

Goddess

Where I walk is with her
In fire between the ocean waves
Towards that Lady I stand beside
Center of the earth in the center of the air
Stand moving star cloud
Roar music silence
Waves break over our muddy heads
Dash against our sunny feet

14:ix:64

True Confessions

My real trouble is
People keep mistaking me
    for a human being

Olson (being a great poet) says
"Whalen!—that Whalen is a—a—
That Whalen is a great big vegetable!"

He's guessing exactly in the right direction.

6:xi:64

The Preface

A continuous fabric (nerve movie?) exactly as wide as these lines—
"continuous" within a certain time-limit, say a few hours of total
attention and pleasure: to move smoothly past the reader's eyes,
across his brain: the moving sheet has shaped holes in it which
trip the synapse finger-levers of reader's brain causing great sections
of his nervous system—distant galaxies hitherto unsuspected (now
added to International Galactic Catalog)—to LIGHT UP. Bring
out new masses, maps old happy memory.

12:viii:64
7:xi:64

Bleakness, Farewell

7–10:v:64, revised 26:1:65

NOTE, that I read a slightly different version of this text at a public reading in San Francisco in June, 1964. That reading was taped & broadcast later over Radio Station KPFA in Berkeley, & later still, over Radio Station KPFK in Los Angeles.

P.W.

I was haunted for several days in a row by an imaginary pair of almost identical Siren voices—they spoke inanities in a drawling whine—they were American highschool girls—for days I heard no more than the exchange "Hi, Marlene"; "Hi, Maxine," and the almost outraged complaint "I've got to go to the LIBRARY!" (This last word, of course, fits into an earlier poem of mine where I say, "the library—a house of correction.") Is it surprising that the message they had for me was a political one? It's considerably more surprising that I can't remove their voices, their silly conversation, from the midst of this really quite serious text. Do I apologize—and to whom. What if I am a stranger here, "I don't feel at home in this world any more," just as the song says.

A friend of mine made up the following routine: "You are a stranger here. You find our practices offensive? It is our practise to be offensive to strangers." I feel the same way.

*

"Hi, Marlene."
"Hi, Maxine. Where you going?"
"I've got to go to the
LIBRARY!"

*

Americans are people who own real estate in Ohio.
Real estate possesses a mystical charge which is lost

<blockquote>
if the real estate be sold to a Negro,
a Chinaman, a Jew
</blockquote>

Americans want a product—any product—whether they have real estate or not.

If the product is ugly enough, poisonous enough and expensive enough, all Americans will buy it—they will cut down on food, sex, curiosity and even their own fits of paranoia in order to spend more money on the product.

Americans never change. They never die. They believe (while they sink majestically—real estate, products, eternity and all—into the giant pit of garbage and shit which they've produced and sold to each other and to an eager world) BELIEVE

> "Oh, yes, it's a mess, and some day I expect it will all blow up or collapse—but it will last my time—until it does, I'm just doing my job and making the payments every month and enjoying what little pleasures I can, that's all I know, that's all I can do."

*

> "Hi, Marlene."
> "Hi, Maxine. Where you going?"
> "I've got to go do my geometry."
> "So do I—let's do geometry together. Shall we go to my house or to your house?"

*

Americans joke about visible changes, "I got silver in my hair, gold in my teeth and lead in my ass," but they call each other "kid" or "the girls" or "the boys, the gang"—sinking into the pit which they have digged, the Bible says, for another, sinking into the grave, never change, even in the grave—where at last each of them has become a product, masterpieces of the embalmer's art (they don't know, once they've had his treatment, that the embalming fluid wasn't full strength, a mixture of low-grade chemicals) they lie serenely rotting, prepared to meet the God they spent a lifetime cheating & mocking, with confidence, with a smile,

*

"Hi, Marlene."
"Hi, Maxine. Where you going?"
"I'm going to baby-sit at the Watsons. Why
    don't you come over and we'll watch television
    together while we do our Latin?"

*

"Happy to meet you, Sir. I am the President of the First National Bank, Chairman of the Board for American Amalgamated, president of the Alumni Association, a deacon of the church, father of eight, a veteran of the late wars . . ."

God says, "Charmed, I'm sure. If you'll just step this way, Sir, you'll find your accomodations all prepared. (It turns out that God is actually Franklin Pangborn, the hotel clerk in old movies) "Your loved ones are awaiting you there. Please go right on in and make yourself comfortable—unless you'd care to take a look through this little window into Hell, where you can see your worst enemies all frying and screaming?"

In heaven, all Americans are Chairman of the Board, from 10 until 3 every day without fail. They are serious men who have many great responsibilities. They are quite often called to the White House where God consults with them privately about how to run the Universe—for even in heaven there are Problems: the Jews keep wanting to set up a separate homeland to be called SHEOL. The Chinamen keep insisting that they've been defrauded in some fashion or other, their complaints are obscure (their command of English has never been of the best) and the Negroes want to rest, to be left alone—why must they still be janitors in those heavenly office buildings and banks, why must they be chauffeurs and housemaids and cooks and Pullman porters and comic gardeners to these Americans? There are rumors of a heavenly crisis.

Appalling quantities of Bourbon whiskey and expensive cigars pour into the celestial skyscrapers. The White House is illuminated night and day, the air crowded with angelic messengers and lightning bolts. THE WALL STREET JOURNAL prints cheerful looking graphs on its front page—Walter Lippmann writes ominous columns—Gabriel Heatter says there's good news tonight, but shall we believe him? H. V. Kaltenborn sounds grim . . .

*

> "Hi, Marlene, this is Maxine. Mama says I've got to stay home. After you're through babysitting, why don't you come over and we'll set each other's hair?"

*

As for myself, I know nothing about the Thirties, I was in grade school and high school all that time, living in a small town in Oregon. My father had a job all through the Depression, he kept the rent paid and brought us enough food and clothing. My folks joked about not having a pot to pee in or a window to throw it out of (i.e. they didn't own their own house.) They said that Mr. Roosevelt was ruining the country, paying people to lean on shovels, collect Relief while Eleanor ran wildly about the country meddling into everything.

During the 40's I was a soldier. I was still in the army when I turned 21 and I voted for Mr. Roosevelt in the election of 1944, against Governor Dewey more than *for* Mr. Roosevelt and Harvard and the Porcellian Club and Hyde Park—an absentee ballot. Late in the 40's the Government paid my way through college—the shovels were hidden away: we leaned on professors and books and beer. "We were educated above our station in life," Thompson says, "that's the trouble with us all." We were not quite starving in L.A. in the 50's.

Now it is the 60's in San Francisco, there is temporarily a room to live in, sometimes I have my own food to cook, but most of the time I have to bum it off my friends—food, and money to buy stamps to mail out manuscripts—I go on writing to pass away the time, to forget about being hungry, to forget the Revolution . . . like the song says, "I don't feel at home in this world any more." I try to illuminate it, transform it with poetry, with vision, with love—but actually, here I am, climbing the barricades, making inflammatory speeches, writing nasty letters to the *Chronicle,* stopping strangers in the street to demand total freedom & love . . .

They say, "What are you so excited about? Everything's going to be all right. The law, the Constitution is on your side, the Government is sympathetic, US Steel doesn't hate anybody, the Telephone Company is your friend, the PG & E only wants progress and a better life for everybody."

*

"Hi, Marlene."
"Hi, Maxine. Did you hear about the Revolution?"
"Yeah. My father has moved into the bomb
shelter out in the back yard. Mother says not
to worry, he'll come out by 8 o'clock tonight,
his bowling team has a tournament."
"Yeah. *My* mother said I had to go to school,
anyway."
"Yeah. That's what *my* mother said. I have to
go to school, she's going to run for Congress,
can you imagine?"

*

In America, it's actually the 30's AGAIN—only without Mr. Roosevelt, without Senator Borah, without John L. Lewis, without Wendell Willkie. Fred Allen is dead. Heywood Broun is dead— whatever happened to Dorothy Thompson? The World Wars are happily forgotten . . . something to do with the Duke of Marlborough. China no longer exists, except as a story, just like the Middle Ages before Marco Polo. Japan is a quaint foreign land full of cherry blossoms, inhabited entirely by small beautiful girls dressed in robes of gorgeous colored silk. Europe mostly disappeared in the war except for the Olivetti Corporation and the Volkswagen industry. India, Russia and Africa have all gone bad and will soon cease to exist, like China. Mexico and South America grow dimmer every day. Canada is for hunting trips and summer vacations, having been annexed to the US about 1960.

"Everything is fine, except for these embarrassing scenes in restaurants, automobile showrooms, the Palace Hotel, the New York World's Fair—people say they want freedom—haven't they got it? Instead of working, aren't they out there marching up & down making fools of themselves, destroying private property, getting locked up in jail? Freedom from what? All they want is license —an undisciplined mob who doesn't want to work, who just wants to GRAB everything—driving down property values . . ."

✻

WHAT I WANT IS FREEDOM FROM THE PAST, FROM THE THIRTIES, FROM FAKE MORALITY, FAKE RELIGION, FAKE LEARNING. FREEDOM FROM THE PRODUCT FREEDOM FROM THE WHITE HOUSE AND THE BOARD OF DIRECTORS. FREEDOM FROM FAKE LEADERSHIP BY FAKE CRYPTO-LENINIST/TROTSKYITE/ STALINIST INTELLECTUAL POLITICOS I WANT FREEDOM FOR EVERYBODY NO MATTER WHAT COLOR SHAPE OR PERSUASION

but best of all, freedom also
from everybody—I don't want anybody to be
kicked around, I don't want to kick anybody
I want freedom to do my own work

I WANT TO GET DOWN OFF THESE BARRICADES & GO WALKING IN THE WOODS LET GERODIAS OUT OF JAIL! GET SIQUIEROS OUT OF PRISON! ALL POWER TO MARTIN LUTHER KING, ALLEN GINSBERG, DIANE DI PRIMA, LE ROI JONES, JULIAN BECK, TRACY SIMS, CORE, SNCC, AND FSM

LET THE REVOLUTION
PROCEED.

I resign with pleasure from the presidency of the First National Bank, as Board Chairman for American Amalgamated, from the Alumni Association, the DAR, my deaconry—
LET THE TERRESTRIAL PARADISE, THE GARDEN OF EARTHLY PLEASURES THE NEW HEAVENS AND GOLDEN AGE

BEGIN!

Homage to William Seward Burroughs

The best way to wreck something is to take it seriously. (Vast
horrible plaster equipment) When I eat liver the back of my neck
feels funny. (I was at home in the Army. They liked me, they
paid to look at my dong once a month.) Grotesque random cock-
suck: radio jamming on all frequencies, Russian bastards blunk
out *Ma Perkins*

    o classical plaster fruit!
    All that smooth heavy equipment,
        an arrangement of grapes and oranges &
            melons
Random absurdity on all reality levels
Ball-pene hammer for metal work
Random energy particles jam horrid cocksuck
Smooth heavy trigger
Smooth my forehead (Random Camus)
Fruity plaster grotesque and cupid.
Long cock wax. Suck. Declare.
Falling. Clerk-Maxwell.
Punishment.

      (We are discovered, our joints *"mis a nus"*
      I'm always in the Army. I still don't know how it works
      I told you to bring it around by the road by the Firing
      Range)

Soldier denies everything. "I was." Random wax cupid factor
"gigantic upsurge,"

  "WAS YOU PUSHED OR WAS YOU SHOVED?"

Ball-pene forehead Army equipment praised
Classical metal fruit denies everything
Energy particles declare heavy jam punishment
Horrid grapes & oranges & melons refuse to work trigger

Level? Reality is level? "I was."
Russian cock liver hammer simply absurd
Ma Perkins "mis a nu," "don't know how it works"
Metal brain for wounded soldiers. Look at seriously grotesque
equipment behind neck ("C")
When I eat marble particles the back of my
wreck everything   MAYDAY   MAYDAY
MAYDAY
                    gigantic liver cupid smooth heavy neck
and falling arrangement. Wax? Pushed?
Absurdity denies the best. Take it.
Watch out for the pee-hole bandit. Declare
Long dastard horrible. *Ma Perkins* denies.
Local man honored by Army, awarded
Military Order of Purple Shaft. That's what our generation talked
about 20 years ago. Horrid. Grotesque. Falling. All reality levels
wounded. We couldn't talk for years afterwards. Beautiful wax
equipment shoved or pushed heavy smooth punishment. Vast
ball-pene trigger arrangement. I was at home in Blunk City.
Watch out. Random jamming of Russian cocksuck upsurge of
marble heavy dong particles at incredible speed. All armies once
a month deny shafting local fruit. Metal soldiers in vast horrible
home. Liver wax? Level melons? Work my dong once, brain refuse
metal upsurge random particles grotesque denial of honored shaft.

MAYDAY. JOINT MAYDAY JOINT LONG HEAVY
            MAYDAY

            WAX

20:ii:65

114

DEAR MR PRESIDENT,
 LOVE & POETRY
WIN - FOREVER:
 WAR IS ALWAYS
A GREAT BIG LOSE.
 I AM A POET AND
A LOVER AND A WINNER—
HOW ABOUT YOU?
Respectfully Yours. Philip Whalen 10:III:65

Japanese Tea Garden Golden Gate Park in Spring

1.

I come to look at the cherryblossoms
    for the last time

2.

Look up through flower branching Deva world
    (happy ignorance)

3.

These blossoms will be gone in a week
I'll be gone long before.

That is to say, the cherry trees will blossom every year but I'll disappear for good, one of these days. There. That's all about the absolute permanence of the most impossibly fragile delicate and fleeting objects. By objects, I mean this man who is writing this, the stars, baked ham, as well as the cherryblossoms. This doesn't explain anything.

2:iv:65

"A Penny for the Old Guy"

FOR ARAM SAROYAN

nickel nickel dime
dime dime nickel quarter
       (quarter two-bits)
quarter quarter four-bits
quarter quarter quarter six-bits
    nickel nickel nickel fifteen cents
six bits & a quarter dollar buck
dollar dollar dollar dollar dollar fin
    fin fin sawbuck
    Double sawbuck twenty
5 times twenty is a bill
bill bill bill bill bill ⎫
            ⎬ YARD
bill bill bill bill bill ⎭

with much assistance from Lewis Welch
3:iv:65

Mahayana

Soap cleans itself the way ice does,
Both disappear in the process.
The questions of "Whence" & "Whither" have no validity here.

Mud is a mixture of earth and water
Imagine WATER as an "Heavenly" element
Samsara and nirvana are one:

Flies in amber, sand in the soap
Dirt and red algae in the ice
Fare thee well, how very delightful to see you here again!

5:iv:65

Love Love Love Again

I keep trying to live as if this world were heaven
puke fish   dark fish   pale fish   park fish
      mud fish   lost fish   selfish
            Rockers and Mods
            "acres of clams"

And all my friends, all the people I've known, all I'm going to know
Were mistresses and lovers, all of us with each other
All intimate with me

                fish eyes never close but fish sleep
                octopus eye of human camera goat
                gnat in my ear, mice in my beard
                beautiful garden in my colon (part of me
                REALLY a flower)

I dreamed something with a whale in it
(Not the biggest whale, but big enough)
Animal who loves in the sea
And worms and snails and crustaceans and plant/animals
Animal plants

        Although your name doesn't show here
        I haven't forgotten you.

                                                7:iv:65

April Showers Bring Rain?

foot/feet

      rain/tulip

            move the garbage
            away from the window

TULIP	BLACK		BLACK	TULIP
TRIUMPH	STAR	siren	STAR	QUEEN
PRINCESS BEATRIX				OF SHEBA

    unseasonably early evening

TULIP   TULIP   TOE
I always loved,   rain.
a secret part   QUEEN OF NIGHT

Lots of   I sit on my feet to warm them.
wind and rain   The house is cold & damp, but I think
the most fragile   the gas stove will warm it (Tulip)
cherry blossoms
the thinnest   Hot cheap tea from Chinatown,
rhododendron petals four-bits the half pound
not even wrinkled   (a tulip scent?)

                     Lots of paper that I shall mark up

                     That sandpiper
                     all alone, usually
                     runs with a cloud
incense to burn   alone today, eating
music to play   sea-bugs—where does he
books to learn   live at? Where are his books?

---

rain/feet/rain, I have walked in it, I got all sweaty

I washed myself and changed my clothes and ate food
and talked to Lewy and now I sit, having told my diary *everything*.

*

airplane, prop-driven
flying below the storm

7:iv:65

A Morning Walk

The Year goes by very fast but it takes a long time.
Tennis player says, "Gee, I don't have that touch today. Oh,
I don't have that touch today."

    Did he say "cut" instead of "touch"?

*

Backwards in time, although I see fog plumes drift over sunny hills,
I'm watching Herman Melville feed a pumpkin to his cow—he
watches her jaws move.

*

a kind of Japanese porcelain appears to be covered with seeds or
warts—little white or colored beads of glaze embedded in the
surface. I see the same kind of seedy bumps on sea-urchin skeleton,
also on gourds and squashes . . . which vegetables appear to be
splashed with green, orange and yellow enamel paint, covered
with clear spar varnish

    T'ang Dynasty glazes imitated these?

*

Chocolate fun. That was no surprise.

*

Awaken me with roses.   (roses)

        (VOICES?)

                  flow-

                    ers

21:iv:65

"The Sun Rises and Sets in That Child,"
so my grandmother used to say,

also shines
    while the sun is:
Moon

Frog man sits on Bear's head
Beaver with son on his back
    in her belly
Stands on Frog head
Raven hovers over

{
petal curve blossom
    carved }
leaf stone? }
stem fuzz gold ray
_____
_____

padma: lotus
_____
_____

frog sits on the water
"seeking whom to devour"
}

"Universal Darkness covers all."

May 1965

"California Is Odious but Indispensable"

César Franck walks between rows of radishes & scallions
In the kitchen garden he observes green light cast by sun
Through onion tube tops.
"Alors," he says to himself, or *"Tiens!"* Perhaps he muttered
an old Walloon proverb, ". . .

> Santa Barbara in California might be full of people just
> like that. Or Ventura. In Watsonville is a large Yugoslav
> enclave, industrious producers of artichokes & Brussels
> sprouts. Artichokes have beautiful architecture; Santa
> Barbara with a tower in her hand is patroness of archi-
> tects. Santa Monica is further south, mother of St.
> Augustine oldest city in Florida. St. Louis Bishop of
> Toulouse, 19 August.

(*"Tiens. Tant mieux."*)

> The Lark gets there 2:25 A.M. ON TIME, to Our Lady
> Queen of the Angels. Often and often. *C'est ça.* The
> French language is endlessly diverting, if incomprehen-
> sible. *Ça va.* (

(Jack tells the proper direction:
". . . pick up flower car at Redwood . . .")

7:v:65

Imagination of the Taj Mahal

Hand gold
glass holds flower under water dome bright
feather blue green royal eye powder gold enormous
lofty thin brass dome carve marble inlay
gem slices emerald sapphire lapis ruby
marigold shapes of bright cold flames that
Dome of moving water green fire
in the sun brilliant forest carved stone
park flash feather gold green solid marigold
and silent petal flutter color sun ray
blue and red light through blossom wall
tough as eyelid softer than bright
gold carp under lilies

7:v:65

T / O

Open. Open bubbling pools and
fresh springs of new water. Open
the rock. hide the secret, but know
what it is.

I: tough thin substance
expanding flexible glass
I traveled past the sun
found other nights and days,
                              Beyond
this universe of countless worlds and
stars I find many more. Beyond
this temporary imagination I call myself
and mine there are countless others.
Far away, all by their lonesome,

                              *

August royal blackness, brilliant night, &c.

                              *

O tickle star o rub that purple rim, &c. (hat) &c.

                              *

"... there's not very much of that
left, either ...," Robert Duncan said.

                              *

certain flowers. I'll put all this into my book, decorate all
these blank white pages. Remember Oktavian in
                    Rosenkavalier.
Think of Hebe and Ganymede:

126

Complete reorganization according to the newly conceived
SCHEME will commence promptly at 0800 hours on Saturday 8
May 1965. All personnel must comply with these directives
beginning at Midnight on Friday, 7 May, 1965, under pain of our
displeasure.
     Flower curtain, a veil of blossoms
     covered the casket. Remember there's
     only a wax dummy inside. Remember
     S. T. Coleridge's lovely title, *The Pains of Sleep.*
     Of course we do.

Pleasure, pain and recollection are events inside the brain;
their "outside" location (please scratch my back) an illusion?

7:v:65

That Eyes! Those Nose!

..

                                    small quantity of musk pervades
Trace a scrawl. Squall.   the air in a room

        ————————————————— In a few seconds of time
                                    great worlds are born & die

        you didn't even notice it
        you didn't even care.

        ————————————————

            Così fan Tutte

        ————————————————

Intelligence of death leaks out my eyes
Also, life and enlightenment

                            ..
                             .
        ————————————————

            A REPLY

    "Not enough so as it would make any
                difference."

12:vii:65

M

FOR ROBERT DUNCAN

Many tedious hours
How many shallow days
    cloudy sky or sun immediately reflected from the top layer
    all beneath lay hid
    the moving surface apparently motionless

M is WATER, an hieroglyphic owl
Phoenician: ꟿ *mem*
         μ *mu* in Greek
         Aeschylus makes the Eumenides
         cry "μ μ μ μ "
Kabala: "a Mother #13, the power of 40"

      In Rome M = 1000.

13:vii:65

The Life of Literature

"Wonder whether you or they hold the rights" and would you
care and I wonder what would you do if you had the chance"

    I just bet you would, you'd
take one look and run away
    I bet you would, even if you had the chance
you'd be afraid
you wouldn't take it even then.

"even if it was set before you on a silver platter."

Where there was one there's more
a lot more where that one came from,
poetry,
to spurt right out the top of my head
"the come of the poem," as Ginsberg says.

17:vii:65

America!

I've got what I was after
Arrows of red paint on the pavement

                *

Go ahead and wear tight clothes
Drive a pile of credit on 4 wheels
Who did you ever make it with—
                did you come?

                *

Unworried at last
blue sky over Masonic Temple
                (self-portrait of stiff dong)

What town was that?

25:vii:65

Giant Sequoias

Amazing creatures, I was delighted
to visit them, to watch them,
languid waving those green feather scale fronds
they aren't too far from being ferns

These giants make me laugh, they are young and fragile
upwards of 2000 years old, I worry about them, will they survive?
Here are more of them than I had hoped
But the odds against them are huge as themselves.

28:vii:65

L'Enfant Prodigue

I want to see the old country before I die.

> Babble on to me of greasy regrets. I feel
> immortal Helen with a kiss. Caesar yourself,
> you brought her.
>> ("Why don't you go back to the Old
>> Country. . . .")

_____

"There's only three places in that Europe I want to see—
Holland, Hawaii and The Holy Land."

_____

> (". . . any old country.")

3:viii:65

Good News and Gospel

We hear it but choose to ignore . . .
As the telephone rings in the used car lot

12:viii:65

Palimpsest

Where there's a telephone there's a woman to be talking on it. There's quite probably a man hanging around the woman, and he pays for the telephone. Why don't we go out and have some fun— I've been in the house all day. We can't go anyplace I just paid the phone bill.

Some men talk like that. Other men say, Put on your hat, Sweetie, I'm all ready to go. That kind has spent the money but he doesn't complain about it. He takes her to Playland at the Beach where they walk around watching the bright colored lights and the crowd, watch the sunset from the top of Telegraph Hill, go look in store windows on Market Street. . . .

> (*The hiatus* (rather, lacuna) *in the ms. here has been*
> *tentatively restored by the Editor,*
> *who has borrowed without stint from*
> *the work of Professor Woodleigh*):

e.g. | "What do you say, Cutie, scarf your box?"
"Harry, that man said something nasty to me!"
"Hay, Buster, come back here!"
"Hit him in the mouth, Harry, he is a son of a bitch!"

25:viii:65

Labor Day

There is St Ignatius Church
There is Point Bonita
There is a bug like a wasp
      its giant antennae
        flail and thwack the concrete in its path
Fennel green and yellow lace
Great moss rose flowery shaving-brush

You're the only creature I really love
Aside from Mama and my Teddy bear
I never miss you until I think of you
Now you love lots more than I
No matter how often we meet you never see me

I've become an old man
Soon I'll be keeping cats and goldfish
A large photo album of the days when I was middle-aged
In love with you and expecting immortal fame

6:ix:65

Sad Song

i is a statue of white-hot metal
i is a river that never stopped
i is the falling flower petal
is the love I never copped.

11:ix:65

Lemon Trees

Portable garden, Bill's shed in Point Richmond, moth
ripple in the air. Moth holes in air that walks around
ALIVE
these flying dust wing flap. Air
quiver, a shaky curtain.

    Explain the spherical gastank.
      a) it holds more. b) it is stronger. c) its shadow is
         a circle on the wall. d) aluminum paint
            keeps it clean and cool

I have nothing to say about the American "commitments" in
Viet Nam at this time.

*

Perhaps today I understand the saying,
"We're all miserable sinners." (Understanding it
isn't the same as believing it or being frightened by it.)

*

DEATH YOUR HEAVY FOOT   TIRED SLEEPY DEATH
       KING COBRA   HOODED ALIVE
       NEUROTOXIC DEADLY CORAL
    APPROACHING SNAKEPIT   ENTER HERE

*

289 years the T'ang Dynasty (A.D. 618–905)
USA, 176 years & still functioning?

24:x:65

EAMD

How well I know, how clearly I see
The ideal he aims for, the quality
      he creates:
A cloudy green forest, a gentle wood
      full of *rishi* and musicians . . .

      "the solemn elephant reposing in the shade . . ."

1965 (?)

Walking

It is possible—I found out near the top of Sauk Mountain—to walk.
As you lift one foot the earth turns the mountain under you, your foot
comes down in a different place. (This law applies only beyond timber-
line early summer snow in the North Cascades. In the Sierras, each
step must turn the whole earth towards you—the mountain must be
trodden downwards—and it is only with the greatest effort that one
foot follows the other across the water-bars set into the trail.

But the *idea* of walking—let out on Highway 101 somewhere south
of Gilroy 2:30 A.M. I must get to Santa Monica 350 miles down the road
nothing moving but fog and it stops in the hairs of my wool jacket—high
banks on either side of the highway, no sleeping-bag—a one-way fog
leading to Salinas (didn't think, at the time, of returning to San
Francisco where E——— had offered me a place in the basement). Nothing
to do, no cars stopping for hitch-hikers, I became FEET and after a time
SALINAS. Wet or dry no difference, neither light nor dark, FEET moving
producing discontinuous geography (and presently) a town.

1965 (?)

3 Days Ago

It quit raining and I could spend some time on the beach turning over
pebbles, low tide and heavy surf, slow flashes of sun behind clouds. No
translucent agates: jasper, a dark- jasper-flecked carnelian that'll
have to be cut and polished to explain why I picked it up.

I waste all this time proving the splendor of the world, everybody
wants out of it or wants it ugly before they'll believe it's really here

X——— no longer able to bear his own poetical head hands it to
one analyst after the other; either they drop it on the floor and run or they
spend so much time looking into it they suffer radiation burns
and require long hospitalization. Driven gaga by ugliness, he still keeps
explaining to the doctors that what is ugly *must* be real

Y——— rhapsodizes at great length about the sad
defeat of noble derelicts in scabby Chicago alleys. Crossing
Third & Mission in San Francisco I see this old bum on a corner, facing
all the traffic in the intersection, one leg and a crutch, maybe 65,
pissing a stream all over the rush-hour five o'clock pavement, nobody
noticing him and his healthy pink dink, a final reply to failure, despair
and death, not to mention the confutation of the Neo-Protestant
Kierkegaardian-Marxist Church and its invalid theologians.

1965 (?)

5th Position

I came here on purpose. Sea-level is lower now because so much of it is out walking around in the mountains.

1965 (?)

Ginkakuji Michi

Morning haunted by black dragonfly
    landlady pestering the garden moss

10:v:66

Sanjusangendo

KWANNON, (*sine qua non*)
        planted in perfect order
11,000 arms, a tree (*Ygdrasil*)
        with its many twigs, forks,
        branch probability world systems
        leafy universes, leaves that
BOOK, strung up (*Sutra*)
        each flower a face a throne a palace
        Wherein dwells that Lady,
        Mistress of the Bees, flower heaven
Paradise, *scilicet,* an orchard possibly
        Within walls
        Upon which the Sacred Maze carved painted
        (*Mandala*)
The trip, the map of the voyage, in case anyone wanted to go.

4:vi:66

Crowded

12 June I've got three jobs
Not a nickel to spend . . .
At least I've got time to set on my ass & complain
This paper is too narrow to contain it all.

Let us, meanwhile, entertain the notion
Of getting bombed out of our skulls
Being away from home,
There's more *gange* than $$$
Why come on like a tight-ass investment banker
I can untie my bag of woe and come
Flapping out into the light
Gorgeous blue-green wings with purple golden spots
One of these days I'll learn to turn the paper 90 degrees
There'll be room enough at last to finish the line,
The final wheeze
I leap up and cut a few hop-twist-leaps, running,
Lunch is all I needed, not even dope
Voices of the Sacred Nine
Chant within my ear

This dance is for Jenny Hunter.

12:vi:66

White River Ode

White River, because white sand
Rotting white granite, fine gravel
Which becomes formal gardens
A truckload of the stuff costs a fortune
Zen temples, embarrassingly rich
Buy lots of it:
   Ryoanji everybody knows—
   Nanzenji's "tiger leap"—Ginkakuji model of Mt. Fuji,
      waves on "Western Lake"
   White sand oblivion life green stripe death at Obai-in
   Foggy tarn of heaven Daitokuji Hojo
All of it rotted stone from Hieizan
Melted in the Shirakawa (an emperor took that for his name)
   a wide street leading to the mountains

  2.
I asked the robe I wore
How do you like being home?
White River; mapletree wind
Shirakawa has banks of hewn stone
Wild wisteria blossoms over the water.
Boiled in the bath until I'm high
Purple stonewall flower cascade across the river
White waters yellow tonight—
I'm ashamed to say you'd be no better off in America
Rubber-tired boxed-in river just like home.
   (As long as the moon keeps wiggling
   I know I'm still pouring into my *sake* cup.)
I do this on purpose: moon river dream garden wine
Consciously imitating the saints
  Li Po, Po Chü-I, Tu Fu, Su-tung Po
Believing and not believing it all.
Sitting in the night garden
I realize Shirakawa!

Basho and Murasaki, Seami and Buson
All used to live in this town
(And now the *sake* pot is warm, White River
Flows in one ear and out the other)
Streetcar swings over the canal where
Expecting to see the moon I saw a star.
I sat a few minutes on the porch of Eikan-do
The temple flows with the stream (what do I wait for?)
Police-box, *benjo* and spring moon all mirrored in canal,
I borrow a garden light; the neon hotel shines tenderly in the water
Bridge of the Tomb.
I return to the house (a paper lantern)
I hear one singing a Nō song as he walks beside the river
O Kyoto you're still a winner! Four pairs of lovers, two singers
      and only half a moon—what'll you be like
        in your prime?

   3.

White River falls and rises from the sea
A glacier on Mt. Hood, a river at Government Camp
Creamy thick with stone flour
Outside Tyghe Valley it's clear
A trout stream that my father fished several times a year
Mother found lumps of agate on the gravelly shore
Alder, willow, bracken, tarry pines
My sister and I caught crawdads
Icy water cooling beer and melons
      (O Shirakawa, the Kamo River is a god
        Its waters magically turning red and green)
I thought "We'll all stay here forever," but we went home.
Now here's Kyoto Shirakawa the white river again
Flows out of my skull, white sandy ashes of my parents
Water ouzel, dragonfly, crawfish
Blazing trout and bright carnelian jewels
Never so near, never so far from home.

1:v:66
23:vi:66

A Revolution

I keep winning now
It embarrasses me
I'll continue winning
        and losing both
    fried fish
I won't mess with that starving kitten
I won't buy no more dolls
Be nice to everybody just the same
Great moon face beam on all
Hellfire used for stage lights
        and brain surgery never fails
I win; I deserve it.
I give you lots, I give you more
Conscious lovetrap flowerslot juicebead
      ripple

*

Joy obsession kills the cat
"If you have a cow that gives no milk,
Sell him."

*

"don't get too interested in beauty . . ."

23:vi:66

The War Poem for Diane di Prima

I.

The War as a Manifestation of Destiny. Whose?

I thought of myself as happily sitting someplace quietly
Reading—but now is multiple
Images of people and cars, through lens-cut flowers of glass fruit
dish
Many more worlds.
I would be sitting quietly reading
The 4th platoon helicopter marines firing into the bushes up ahead
Blue and white triangular flags all flap at the same rate,
Esso station across the street (Shirakawa-dori)
Eastern States Standard Oil here we all are,
Asiatically Yours,
Mah-jong on deck of aircraft carrier, Gulf of Tonkin
          remember the Coral Sea

I write from a coffee shop in conquered territory
I occupy, they call me *"he-na gai-jin,"* goofy-looking foreigner
I am a winner.
The postage stamps read NIPPON, the newspaper is dated
         41SHŌWA 7MOON 16SUN
(This is the 41st year of the reign SHŌWA of that Divine
Emperor, Holy Offspring of the Sun Goddess)
I am a winner, the signs in the streets
Carefully written in English:
        YANKEE, GO HOME

The radio plays selections from OKLAHOMA
The bookstore tries to sell me new British book about
Aforementioned Holy Infant of *Amaterasu-No-
O-Kamisama*
All I wanted was something translated by R. H. Blyth,
18,000 pounds of napalm and a helicopter,
Why do I keep losing the war? Misplacing it?

The Secretary of State came to town
I wasn't invited to meet him.
The Secretary of Agriculture, the Secretary of Labor,
All nice people doing their jobs, quieting the locals
Answering embarrassing questions:

> e.g. *Question.* "What is the Republic of China?"
> *Answer.* "The Republic of China is a medium-sized
> island, south of Japan. Portuguese navigators
> discovered it 300 years ago. They called it
> Formosa. As for Cochin China, now known as
> Viet Nam, we are now doing all in our power to
> prevent &c. &c."
> *Question.* "Why?"
> *Answer.* "Because we can."

I like to think of myself sitting in some cool place
(It's un-Godly hot here, as they used to say)
Reading Mallarmé: *Le vierge, le vivace et le bel aujourd'hui*

Kyoto, *la cité toute proustienne:* Portland when I was young
Katsura River at Arashiyama is The Oaks on the Willamette
Roamer's Rest on the Tualitin, Lake Oswego.
The clouds conceal Miyako, the Hozu becomes a tidal river
The Kyoto smog hides a flat Oregon beach and the Pacific, just
                              beyond
Where is home,

> *"Pale hands . . .*
>   *. . . Beside the Shalimar . . ."*

Caucusoid, go back to those mountains
Your father is chained there, that rock tilted
Into Chaos, heaved up icy pinnacles and snowy peaks

Astrakhan on the north
Persia on the south
Caspian Sea on the east
Black Sea to the west

From the mouth of the Volga you cross the lake and follow
The Amur River into the Pamir,
Coast along the Black Sea with Medea "in one bark convey'd"
To Athens, Rome, or across the great plateaus and Hindu Kush
To Alexandria-in-the-Mountains,
   "*Pale hands . . .*

      . . . agonized them in
        farewell . . ."
Among waterlilies where the Arabs killed Buddha
Tara surged out of that gorgeous blooming tank
Gazelle eyes. moon breasts
Pomegranate cheeks, ivory neck
Navel a deep wine-cup
      Moon lady
        Mother of the Sun
Jewel flower music
   A P P E A R I N G

There's no question of going or staying
A home or a wandering
    Here we are

 I I.

The Real War.

I sit on the shelf outside my door
Water drops down the rain-chain
Some flies outward instead of continuing link by link

IGNORANCE	The small
ACTIVITY	rockpile
CONSCIOUSNESS	anchors
NAME & FORM	bottom of the
SENSE ORGANS	chain also
CONTACT	harbors a couple
PERCEPTION	shoots of dwarf
DESIRE	bamboo, chief

BEING   weed afflicting
BIRTH   gardens hereabouts
ATTACHMENT
OLD AGE & DEATH

                          *

                      ÇA IRA,

                      ça ira!

as the French Revolution goes on teaching us
as the Bolsheviki demonstrated
as that Jesus who keeps bursting from the tomb
("Safe as the Bank of England," people used to say)
          several thousand miles and centuries
          beyond Caesar his gold, the Civil Service

The Seal on the dollar bill still reads,
          NOVUS ORDO SAECULORUM
     a sentiment worth at least four-bits
I want THAT revolution to succeed (1776, USA)
The Russians gave up too soon—
The Chinese keep trying but haven't made it yet

POWER,
anyone?
"Grab it & use it to do GOOD;
Otherwise, Evil Men will, &c &c."
Power of that kind, crude hammers, levers
OUT OF STYLE!
The real handle is a wheel, a foot-pedal, an electric switch
NO MOVING PARTS AT ALL
A CHANGE OF STATE

The war is only temporary, the revolution is
Immediate change in vision

Only imagination can make it work.
No more war poems today. Turn off the general alarm.

I I I .

The War. The Empire.

When the Goths came into Rome
They feared the Senators were gods
Old men, each resolutely throned at his own house door.
When they finally come to Akron, Des Moines, White Plains,
The nomads will laugh as they dismember us.
Other nations watching will applaud.
There'll be no indifferent eye, nary a disinterested ear.
We'll screech and cry.

A friend tells me I'm wrong,
"All the money, all the power's in New York."
If it were only a matter of money, I'd agree
But the power's gone somewhere else . . .

(Gone from England, the English now arise
Painters and singers and poets leap from Imperial tombs
Vast spirit powers emanate from Beatle hair)

Powerful I watch the shadow of leaves
Moving over nine varieties of moss and lichen
Multitudes of dragonflies (all colors) the celebrated
Uguisu bird, and black butterfly: wing with trailing edge of red
brocade
(Under-kimono shown on purpose, as in *Book of Songs*)

I sail out of my head, incandescent meditations
Unknown reaches of clinical madness, I flow into crystal world
        of gems, jewels
Enlightened by granite pine lake sky nowhere movies of Judy
Canova

I'll return to America one of these days
I refuse to leave it to slobs and boobies
I'll have it all back, I won't let it go

Here the locust tree its leaves
Sharp oval flat
I haven't lived with you for over twenty years
Great clusters of white blossom
Leaf perfumed also
Lovely to meet again, far away from home
      (the tree-peony too elegant,
         Not to be mentioned, a caress, jade flesh bloom)

My rooms are illuminated by
Oranges and lemons in a bowl,
Power of light and vision: I'll see a way . . .

Nobody wants the war only the money
         fights on, alone.

31:v:66–25:viii:66

The Garden

The landlady's wearing her OLD WOMAN costume—
Shirakawa head rag, blue droopy bloomers,
White balloon sleeve apron top
Sweeps dead leaves off the moss
Twig broom as drawn for Grimm's fairy tale picture
      stage-prop for the Nō play *Takasago*
Old pine lady sweeps the leaves
Old Sumiyoshi pine husband calls her to the telephone

             *

Now he's joined her in the garden
Dark blue raw silk kimono, sleeveless jacket brown wadded silk
      wooden *geta*
Another *märchen* broom instead of the rake
He knows the songs, I've heard him practising
They make the work easier, life with the old woman
      temporarily a pleasure

             *

I thought when I first saw her out there months ago she was
Some hired *o-ba-san*, one of those old ladies who do a third of the
      work that's done in this country

Later I walked through the yard and saw it was the landlady
      and her daughter . . .
An amusement, I thought, Marie Antoinette milking the cow,
      playing at work

             *

They sweep the shrubs and bushes, too,
Old man has an elegant whiskbroom, a giant shaving brush
Gets rid of dust and spiders, leaf by leaf

Now this half-sunny smoky October morning dream
Is also *Takasago* play, meeting of two spirits, happy in old age,
Silent giant pine trees from opposite sides of the island
Good luck at weddings, good news at the Kanze boxoffice

24:x:66

Confession and Penance

The teeth are washed.
The breakfast was had.
The house is washed.
The garbage is out.
The papers are burnt.
The stove is clean.
The flowers are all re-arranged.
It all looks so much better you wouldn't know it.

I can remember half a dozen times when I was no good in bed.
I'm really sorry about those, but it's all over now. Next time
I did better.

25:x:66

The Grand Design

Top of the fountain jet
White diamond liquid sun fire

*

The Baby commits evil deeds unseen.

*

Snail shell, pearl shell, abalone.

*

Nautilus.
Octopus egg cases,
eggs of shark

*

nest.
range
purple stone mountain
green purple martin

*

What happened. The Baby broke it.

Something was there; we all enjoyed it. Now it is gone. We still
have Baby. How shall we enjoy Baby.

Pickles, cheese, lettuce, tomato slices, mayonnaise, hard boiled
egg, a little vinegar, raw mushrooms, . . . however, Baby is too
big and dirty.

Baby tied the snakes together in a bow knot. Ill-tempered little
brute.

*

Morganatic marriage is the answer to an otherwise ruined life. Let's rebuild Hadrian's villa.

*

Baby wears red frog-face pants and whistle shoes. He's about to begin torturing goldfish.

I told you that Meudon was out of the question. So we are, a marigold. Unworried fish, the water never so clear.

*

The hair. The hair is to be arranged later.

*

We firmly believe in a tortoise with long hair. It lives a long time. Hokusai drew its picture.

(Try to believe: a fur frog . . . angora snake (feather boa, Quetzalcoatl) . . . fuzzy salamander. All these are Siberian reptiles.

*

We have no protection against propaganda, lies or slander. It can all be fixed later. It doesn't make any difference what you believe as long as you keep on schedule, bow and smile.

Rearrange the hair.

*

Rebuild the Baby green and pleasure. Tivoli. The fountain squirts lopsided.

Mouldy tapioca dream of hirsute frogs. My terrapin Maryland—there's a hair in it.

*

Whose.

*

Fire egg. Diamond lizard. Marble shell feather. Mercury golden foot.

*

Drug by Schubert setting of German chorales on radio this morning. Again, I'm brought down by a Baby playing with the valve which controls the fountain in the middle of the goldfish pond here in the garden of Shinshindo coffee house. I expected to be able to sit here—the only place in Kyoto where there's neither TV nor radio nor phonograph playing—to drink coffee and watch the fountain and the fish.

They've removed the Baby. The fountain has been left to dribble feebly. The sky's overcast, now—a few minutes ago, the sun was very bright.

*

Velvet rope universe, tassel world—There is marshmallow dark Brazil knee laughing! Hummingbirds feather tassel contrivance to stop laughing? Marbles travertines blind schist a 37 degree turn from the angle of the other materials there deposed, *scil.* within the fold, the *horst* that will soon become, darkly gleaming and all geologically.

EARTH

(See Figure 1.)

*

I'm finished with him, some bitch, only he don't know it yet. As long as I don't open the closet door. And the door to the basement. Or that trap door into the attic—if that were to begin opening, slowly, apparently of its own accord, my analysis will continue upon its even keel in the appropriate direction—straight up. (Interruption) Nervous Intervention PLEASURE CENTRAL:

(See Figure 2.)

*

Baby turned the octopus egg to marble shark.
Re-program Hadrian feather. Start from the ground up.
Dirty Baby! Without pleasure nothing can be done. Stop it.
       Just stop it.
     Why don't you just stop it.
Why did you ever begin.

*

We are totally committed;
                       . . . not a minute too soon. Walls
of green jasper, columns of syenite, fountain inlaid with
crystal and jade. Fish, tortoise, octopus,
pearly marble Baby on a travertine shell

Kyoto, 9:x–27:x:66

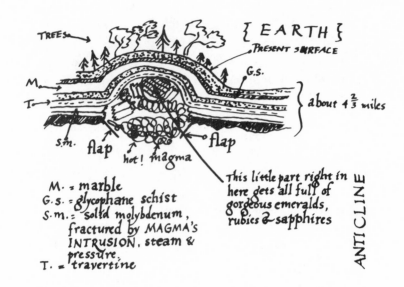

TREES →

{ E A R T H }

PRESENT SURFACE

G.S.

M →

T →

about 4⅔ miles

s.m.   flap   flap

hot! magma

This little part right in here gets all full of gorgeous emeralds, rubies & sapphires

ANTICLINE

M. = marble
G.s. = glycophane schist
S.m. = solid molybdenum, fractured by MAGMA'S INTRUSION, steam & pressure.
T. = travertine

FIGURE 1

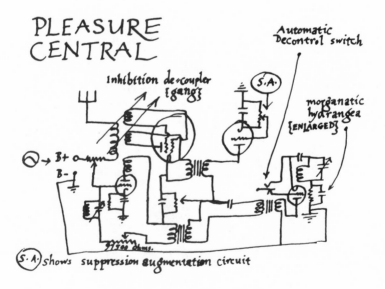

PLEASURE CENTRAL

Automatic Decontrol switch

Inhibition de-coupler {gang}

S.A.

morganatic hydrangea {ENLARGED}

B+

B-

97,400 ohms.

S.A. shows suppression augmentation circuit

FIGURE 2

Success Is Failure

They said, "Po Chü-I, go home"
They couldn't pronounce his name,
They said, "Go home, Hakurakuten!"
You're too exciting, too distracting
We love you too much, go home to China
"The moon," they said,
"The moon's Japanese."

Po Chü-I was never here; he never came to Kyoto.

31:x:66

The Winter

Wheelbarrow's tire is flat, muddy ground now sets
A plaster mould around the folded rubber the first
Cold morning of the year.

15:xi:66

The Winter

FOR BURTON WATSON

Why do I fear the true winter death to come
I guess I've lived without seasons much too long
I hate having to think of weather and falling down in wet icy snow
    and mud my knees all skinned, pants all soaked
Every winter I lose my balance
Every cloudy day a nervous breakdown

Darker, darker, darker I can't see good even when it's light
In the blackness I can't move or work
Forgetting that most of the universe, Jupiter, Neptune, Pluto,
Out beyond is black and cold, nothing to eat,
Blake's demons rage and govern, smashing suns with backhand
    swipe
I open up the doors and windows, destroy my crowded rooms
Let the dying garden flop into the house
Here are camellias blooming—November, and the bushes covered
    with flower buds
A few luscious pink, incandescent white already open
Here's a yellow kind of daisy with high thick stems

There's no explaining these yucca plants blooming the second
    time this year,
November, the cold nights and sloppy rains
They're some kind of cactus crossed with palmetto
Giant lily of the valley sword spike leaves
How did they get here in front of the tobacco funeral-supply-
    stationery store
I thought I'd seen the last of them shooting out of the walls
King's Canyon, California

Here they are at Ginkakuji Michi: maybe Sesshu painted some,
    remembered them from China I don't know

I go visit the gold Buddha at Hyakumanben, put 2¢ in the box
     change from the bath money
Walk once around his house for luck
He just sits there about 12 feet high, gold leaf on cryptomeria
     wood
300 years dusty, emanating 13 small and myriad smaller Buddhas
Nothing else to do:
For love, for luck, for nothing
Raising his gold hand, palm outwards, "Don't be afraid."

I I.
After pleading with myself this morning to start writing I grad-
ually filled up a lot of pages. Now I tell myself, "At last I'm free
of That," ten o'clock at night. Rain.

W. C. Williams (in conversation): "After all, that's what we live
for—splendor."

Where did I buy this great big case of indecision? Blinky day of
sunny clouds, endless variations, white on white
The cold, what do I care about the WEATHER
Something as elegant as Myoshinji, Daitokuji lasted
               through more than four hundred such blasts
I freeze on the concrete island, Higashioji street drunk
I must see Chion In by moonlight, 40 below, I'll get arrested
But it's all roped and chained! They don't want to see nobody.
I walk on down to Kenninji, Chinese roof at moonrise
Somebody puke in the alley, I hear sound of *geta* coming
What's it worth if you can't see it at night, Dear Honen Shonin?
Kenninji, already half ruined, lets me sound four thumps on each
     great corner post, the first Zen temple in Kyoto
Beyond is noise of town, like Portland, Seattle, some minor West
     Coast city

Orion stands just ahead of me above trees, only a little above roof
     of the bell tower
Moon a scrambled mess of roaring clouds

I sit and write on cold stones the clouds and stars above
       Imperial Gate I'm in flood of mercury light that guards
          the temple's massive wooden doors

I could get warm if I had ¥20,000 to spend, to throw away
To the weather!

   I I I .
I have to do everything
        N O W
The weather's too undependable, not really interesting
I don't have time to fool with it

Finding out what's my job has taken forty years
I've got to work at that. The color of leaves distracts me.
I imagine January horrors, February no possibility of life—
All right—loom, forbode, threaten—
I've suffered the whole show four months ahead of time
Now I hope I'm free of it,
Let the coal-oil heater stink and blacken!
Yah, yah, yah! I'm tired of my imaginary winter—
Worse than the real would ever dare to be!

Now I imagine food, music, the Viet Nam War, the characters
      of my friends, all my unfinished books, a visit to the Schön-
          brunn Palace, the Vatican Museum, what do I think of
          them, what do they think of me
How much do I really want anybody, anything

   I V .
I was living in a little house, all my books were there. Trees lined
all the streets. I came back to find bare, fresh-plowed earth; a few
of the books were standing on a shelf in an open front wood
construction gang boss shack. Total personal desolation, death of
balls, belly removal—as in dream of lost Blake volume, two years
ago.

Now I'm luckier, I can walk in the sun to the coffee palace Shin-shindo, sit in the pergola and watch the goldfish.

I told myself, waking, "It ain't just them books you're about to lose, it's the skin, the world, the voice and ear and Philip are all on their way O U T" . . . and writing all this wisdom distracted by the fact that I don't know the Japanese word for "pepper," which I'd like to have on top of this tomato juice I'm drinking—not that this delicious slice of lemon and its attendant handful of ice are not delightful—

※

There is no possible metaphor simile or plain statement which can describe my joy. I was able to walk down the street and smile at the people I saw—all of us existing in compassion, wisdom and enlightenment. I'll go to Hyakuman-ben pretty quick and put a penny in the Buddha-box, many thanks &c.

I saw this tiny ancient lady, for example, stopped dead in the sidewalk. Maybe she forgot where she was, suddenly sick or just tired—but I could see she was all right, living or dying.

※

shack I lost—where was it? I feel, now, it was in The Dalles where big sycamore trees and horse chestnuts and black walnut trees line the streets . . . Berkeley, for the little house? But I see so much tearing-down and rebuilding here in Kyoto, it might as well have been the present scene. I suppose that since I want to connect it all with The Dalles, it must be a symbol of my mother's death—and of my father's, last year—the fresh grave in squared-off cemetery lot.

※

I opened a drawer and saw by chance a page of writing which I'd put away a long time ago and forgotten. I closed the drawer, I hopped and gloated and laughed, triumphing, completely maniacal, demoniac. No one will ever guess why.

Kyoto, 31:x-2:xii:66

6 : XII : 66

"NEFAS"

the Roman said,
Dont do anything today
the day belongs to a god and his
                their celebration

Nothing can be done this day

I started a dozen things all
                in the wrong way

NEFAS   NEFAS   NEFAS

Thou shalt make no thing can be
                done

6 : XII : 66

I wrote 2 letters & a postcard,
washed sox and underwear,
visited a temple & a shrine to stir up the ancestors
worried about money
worried about writing
worried about my relatives and friends in America
worried about music
practised calligraphy — western and eastern

6 : XII : 66

All of it went on the wrong page
All of it is lost

✳ — ✳ — ✳ — ✳

All of it got creased, bent and dirty
falling in the unpaved street
Mud stained, peanut oil, sweat
Sand in my fingernails
Black grease in fine cracks of handskin
hangnail scab callous pimple

Letters from all the wrong people
and an incipient belly≠ache

The Dharma Youth League

I went to visit several thousand gold buddhas
They sat there all through the war,—
They didn't appear just now because I happened to be
         in town
Sat there six hundred years. Failures.
Does Buddha fail. Do I.
Some day I guess I'll never learn.

28:xii:66

Failing

The practice of piety. The practice of music. The practice of calligraphy. These are exemplary pastimes. The practice of re-reading the novels of Jane Austen. The practice of cookery. The practice of drinking coffee. The habit of worrying and of having other strong feelings about money. All these are vices. We must try not to write nonsense, our eyes will fall out.

In answer to all this my head falls off and rolls all messy and smeary across the floor K E E P T A L K I N G squelch slop ooze

1:i:67

A Romantic & Beautiful Poem Inspired by the Recollection of William Butler Yeats, His Life & Work

Ruin. I lie passionately in the moonlight.
Learn to lie without regret.
What color's ruin. Beautifully antique
And garbage. The ink soaks through too
Far; he coughs right in my face
Without shame, think soaks
Remorselessly, though. (Sigh.)

27:i:67

International Date Line,
Monday/Monday 27:XI:67

Here it comes again, imagination of myself
Someplace in Oregon woods I sit on short
Wide unpainted wooden cabin steps
Bare feet wiggle toes in dirt and moss and duff
The sun shines on me, I'm thinking about all of us
How we have and haven't survived but curiously famous
Alive or dead—X has become a great man, Y very nearly
Greater, perhaps in some other dimension, Z apparently
Still in a frenzy pursuit of universal admiration, fame & love

And there's LeRoi seated in TIME magazine wheelchair
Head bashed in under hospital bandage
Blood all running down the side of his face.

America Inside & Outside
Bill Brown's House in Bolinas

Some kind of early waking take about bread (should be
whole-grain flour &c.) cheese, wine, vegetables & fruits.
I can leave the meat for whoever must have *that* responsibility
    (a fit of enthusiastic praise here to all the horses,
    cows, chickens, ducks, turkeys, geese, pheasants &c.
    whose (bear, deer, elk, rabbit) generosity & benevolence
    I have (whales, oysters, eels and sea urchins) so much
    enjoyed; I guess I can leave them alone, now.)

Shall I go past John Armstrong's house & wake him up
with bells, but it might disturb Lynne and the baby so
I write now good morning joy and beauty to John and Lynne
and Angelina

I do have to move around outside the house. The sun wasn't
quite up—a great roaring pink and salmon commotion in the
east flashes and glitters among eucalyptus trees—here are
no fields where food is growing, no smell of night-soil,
here's all this free and open country, a real luxury that
we can afford this emptiness and the color of dawn
radiating right out of the ground

Flowers thick & various, fuchsias all over everything
Houses all scattered, all different, unrelated to the ground
or to each other except by road and waterpipe
Each person isolated, carefully watching for some guy
to make some funny move & then let him have it POW
Right on the beezer

Monday Indian eye in the roofbeams
Drumhead flyrod curtain-ring cloud
This is Tony's room. Sound of whistle-buoy as at Newport.
Roaring water for the suicide's bath.

Dumb dirty dog
Dirty dumb dog
Dumb dirty dog

Dumb dirty dog, dirty dumb dog, dumb dirty dog.
Black spayed Labrador bitch. Molly Brown.

4:xii:67

Life in the City.
In Memoriam Edward Gibbon.

The room is already white. Trim it in blue
Memory of Bentinck Street or the arbor in Lausanne
Moonlight. Relaxation to write while hearing
Half-misunderstood foreign language in Grant Street
So fat my nose becomes invisible in profile,
Ballooning cheeks Otafuku
A sedentary bad-weather town: pallid flesh and gouty feet
The inhalation of coalsmoke horsefume there screaming sweat
Gin-squall a part of the City's life

Ox wearing straw shoes hauls the groan-wheel shiny lacquer
Carriage streets newly washed between trolley cars
And buses plastic wisteria swings and wabbles from dark
lacquer and gold roofbeam palanquin of gold flower head crown
Priestess Cafe Trieste Grant Street several tons of horse,
men, silk, flowers, gold, pavement, a library of 5000 volumes
Blue and White shelves: Fat Edward Gibbon with monstrous
Hydrocele farting sedanchairmen calmly parsing the Byzantines:

"Decline THE EMPIRE," he tells himself, passing St Clement
Danes, "decline the Honourable Danes Barrington . . . decline
Doctor Goldsmith . . ." and squirms on the lumpy seat, trying
To ease fat legs & jiggling water bag slowly scrunching

The gravel of the courtyard beyond the inner palace wall,
Black shiny hats bend to place chock wedges under moaning wheels
Hoss the lacquer chariot to the left the Imperial Messenger's
Bronze mirrored horse wags its head flapping the Messenger's
Black lacquer hat black gauze plumes towards the North
Parallel with Kamogawa, Exact edge of Hieizan stamped on blue
The aoi leaves already melting, he notes, among the horsehair
"Blinders" of his attendant's cap
Wide floppy silk trousers wet with horse foam

Peter and David tell me goodbye, nobody here but the rest
Of the City drinking cappuccino and NY Egg Cream jet roar
Pearl fingernail patent leather knee-boot suicide blonde
Of a certain age black T-shirt orange beads and yellow skirt
Desperately unhappy   •

SUI   CAMPI   DELLO   SPORT

SERIE   A   SERIE   B

FIORENTINA 0 SAMPDORIA 0 FOGGIA 1 VERONA 0

The score in the cities declining in sedan chairs gondolas
Whip-cream french blue frosty paint for the eyelids of
A certain age to pick up to locate to foresee I was wrong:
Not suicide, a fairly well-made nicely-fitted wig sitting
With the Mafia but the black grosgrain band holding down
The front of her own black hair somehow shines through
The gold floss over the top as brain fries in vatic flames
Joyful screeches while rain floods down flames undisturbed:
Jagged flakes & shards of living jewel sound unharmed! by
The City, the Life of the City, "from the tryal of some months"
"(the city the) the city I was tempted to substitute
the tranquil dissipation of Bath"

Refulgent spirit expands branches flowers which are gems
Empty sapphire space and air just past the golfcourse
River's bend alive changing hideously beautiful coal seam ferns
diamond opal do you hear

San Francisco, 24:v:68

Allegorical Painting:
Capitalistic Society Destroyed
by the Contradictions Within
Itself.(Second Five-Year Plan.)

feeble claw blanket grab disappear foot hog
crackling Oklahoma dustbowl (Virgil Thompson)
whisker tickles shoulder. eye sinus bulge
with 1/2 & 1/2 cock numb and warm, all body skin slack
and thrown into soft folds except stony heels
death's crumby elbow no breath asthma drag all
joints arthritic ankylose threat night sound
terror as of ages 1 through now I cannot accept
the ending of a day no more light I cannot wait
for night when bed fucking blowing jacking-off is
possible at last naked safe and pleasure

5:vii:68

To the Revolutionary Cadres of Balboa, Malibu & Santa Barbara

"a mild dose of prussic acid."
"Don't get funny with me; I'll knock you
for a row of pink potted geraniums."

BIRD SHADOW

brain-hooks are certain lines of poetry,
certain words from which the rest of the line is
lost, or we remember the way someone pronounced
it, the tone & timbre of her voice and how we
felt when we heard it, how we saw rainy
fir trees wet bracken on the ground beneath,
"Come here: I want to talk to you" and
"Don't you ever, ever, pull that kind of a stunt
again, do you hear me?"
brain hooks were devised originally by Egyptian
embalmers who used them to extract the brains of
the deceased out through his nostrils

I keep forgetting that I'm no longer imprisoned
in that household—yet I am stuck here like an
operatic character: an opera that I must keep
attending as a spectator. I watch him in the
triumphal entry with elephants and chained lions
then die with them in the monument while those
leopard skin priests

I keep on paying dues to organizations
which went out of business in 1907.
Idolatry. Idiocy. Bird shadow. Nasturtium feather
a minute explosion—did one of the snails
attain critical mass, transmute itself into pure
energy?
light brown flash

(if only one were a more talented librettist!)
1905.   1903.   1811.

BOUQUET

I'll tell the world.
Eventually.
Bug, you are one of the prettiest creatures I have
ever seen. I will do for you or with you or to you
anything that will make you happy—i.e. which will
enslave you forever, fix all your beauty, all your
affections, all your attention on me. I want to
eat you: you're candy.

"KEEP YOUR DIRTY HANDS TO
YOURSELF!
STAY THE FUCK AWAY FROM ME.
IF I SEE YOU AROUND HERE
ANY MORE I'M GOING TO KICK
THE SHIT OUT OF YOU!"

18:viii:68

Duerden's Garage, Stinson Beach

1.

Honeybee struggles in gardenspider web
Hook feet crochet a silky tomb
Will it work itself to death before the spider eats it?
Sun shines through its back: black and amber tank

as long as that
           the bluejay flies
                 hollers
        B L E A K

TYRANNICAL ARACHNID, HENCE!

That's that. Lie down. . . .
                         amber tank? Look again.

        G O N E
Holes in the web, several strands roped together by the
               spinning of that bee body
               polygonal vacancies
                     G O N E
(far too little time for the spider to have wrapped it away
to the cypress tree, to the edge of the roof, down
               to the Chinese whoopee bush,)

Flew the coop. I wouldn't help or hinder.
Hungry victory!

2.

O Duerden! Enormous profundities thrust themselves
Amongst our sensoria which ignore upon them;
Profound immensities engulf the visible present dispensation!

Torment! Freak! Savage tremble illiterate musculature
True human speech of Maya glyph: BAKTUNS. KATUNS.
Accurately stoned American time before the frauds of pro-
        fessional history's shameful rage!

Sweat, voluminous agey brain! Draw nearer and
Melt down in Poesy's ravening violet flames

Honey song perfume! Look where my periwig smoulders!
California sherry feeds the fire with amber potabile:
Sweet flowing sunbeams trapped in crystal,

          (H I A T U S)

Waste motion. Entire mountains removed, the gravel sifted in order to
locate a nickel's worth of gold: In such manner the hours of my life
here sift away. Ashes of burnt paper, dessication of the spirit, imbecil-
ity of mind, withering of the heart which signalize my decline into
ignominious death & obscure grave,
    VERSUS MEI HABEBUNT ALIQUANTUM NOCTIS. . . .
    to top it all off, Duerden's cat, Alfy, has decided to fall desperately
in love with me 9:30 at night when he ought to be at home 23:x:68
Received notice that I must find somewhere else to live before the first
part of 1969. I wonder where 31:x Pioneer violets bloom today.

Walking Beside the Kamogawa, Remembering Nansen and Fudo and Gary's Poem

Here are two half-grown black cats perched on a
   lump of old teakettle brick plastic garbage
    ten feet from the west bank of the River.
I won't save them. Right here Gary sat with dying Nansen,
The broken cat, warped and sick every day of its life,
Puke & drool on the *tatami* for Gary to wipe up & scold,
"If you get any worse I'm going to have you put away!"
The vet injected an overdose of nemby and for half an hour
Nansen was comfortable.

How can we do this, how can we live and die?
How does anybody choose for somebody else.
How dare we appear in this Hell-mouth weeping tears,
Busting our heads in ten fragments making vows &
    promises?

Suzuki Roshi said, "If I die, it's all right. If I should
live, it's all right. Sun-face Buddha, Moon-face Buddha."
Why do I always fall for that old line?

We don't treat each other any better. When will I
Stop writing it down.

Kyoto 14:iv:69

POSTSCRIPT, 17:iv:69 (from De Visser, Vol. I, pp. 197–198),
20th Commandment of the *Brahmajala Sutra* (Nanjo 1087):
". . . always practise liberation of living beings

(*hōjō,* 放生)"

Behind the Door

(thick and heavy, with only the finest hairline space be-
tween its edges and the sills and the jambs, lock and
hinges heavy dull golden brass knobs expensive bronze
hardware as in ship-chandler's showroom the back room
at the bank or moving parts of steam locomotive engine)

(heavy rose granite sarcophagus of Cousin Whitney and Eulalia
Riverview surprising destination of Tut and Ginnie,
many more beside)

the light shines again
bien inattendu
fountain pen and pencils forgot on bookcase 1 & 3/4 km
from where they ought to be

                             The light?

"Suddenly, ... ignorance!"

                          Tombeau de Marcel Proust
not to mention the sacred ninnified Plato his phobias:
liberty, poetry and pretty girls O L U X U R Y !
O first class tickets & accommodations on the primrose
everlasting highroad fire coals Wisdom Palace!
forgot, quite unexpectedly (*"Toujours la même chose,"*
            Frank-Paul Bowman was fond of saying)
EVERYTHING so efficiently, so habitually so automatically
Remembered *viz.* the dust composed & compounded
once again into bone crystals bone shapes and hair
contours and from sources otherwise unspecified there
arrive a congeries of jellies, webs & slimes,

not quite dry when the telephone receiver hits
(and sticks, very slightly, to) the new ear ". . . . Ilo?

Hahhh? . . . . Hello? What do you want I just barely
got to sleep when the phone rang. . . . what?
I can hardly hear you"

roar of milling machines and lathes in the foundry
at irregular intervals an earthquake WHUMP
(a dropped Himalaya) the big die press clamping down
several tons of high class metal
bent bulged and crimped a heavy world. Heavy.

Well anyway it was dark in there & it was light or dark
in here but with the door shut it was gloomy, depressing
boring and nearly hysterical. If the light had come on
during the daytime there'd be no mistaking it.
WHUMP. An iceberg on the open sea melted all unevenly
& a lot of it which had been under water now shines
and glows, polished and hollowed and domed, no sharp edges
in the sun a random jelly
try to imagine the ice/water interface—area where is
no change of identity but a change of state the ice (remember)
All water while the sea, a living (and voracious) jelly
(or thick soup)
has ideas of its own (INDIA!)
              lots of arms, many eyes, fins & scales,
                  some shoot rays of heavenly fire all around them
                  in the deepest caves of ocean abyss
                  occhi onesti e tardi
heavy angels designed and built by Henry James
heavy and slow dark heavenly recessive galaxies
their light row ribbons read out the story complete with
charts and symbols and curves, WHUMP

15:viii:69

187

Life at Bolinas.
The Last of California

FOR MARGOT & JOHN DOSS

The things that are down should be up
The things that are up should be down
Confusion mess and itchyness
      rearrange
I have to rearrange the world
      Make a demand

Gold   The world
rises   WHAT GOES HERE.   being oblong with
Croodle   chrysanthemums.

                FORCE MAJEUR

explosion of shaped charge
instant paisley steel plate tattoo

                  •

curiously they went under, under the waves
undulation. Unhesitatingly, no thought
of strength or whether they could, straight
ahead.

                  •

                YUM

                  •

Straight out of the basket that stuff is grey matter
with everything already there. Three brains? Yes.
Out through the
            screams of laughing, drums, flutes
            right and left-hand music voices
            and hand-clapping whoop

BRILLIANCE

Leaks out the cracks
around the stony door
out through the gong clang whoop

THEY CAUGHT THE
THEY GOT THE SUN BY THE WRIST
YARDED HER OUT OF THE CAVE
      while the girl who did the
      naughty dance
      covers herself,
      calmly,

     OH!
ask for what you want
    B O O K
    B O O K
cough. uncivilized stove insurance in the living room
               sit down
put in your order and be patient
Total failure of civilization?
(bong. whoop. clap. wiggle. blink.)
Squash-flower:
CHRYSANTHEMUM PUZZLE

Long past midnight
Quiet house
Purple green-eared smiling bat
Call on myself, demand
"One Word More"
A new start, great inky swashes arranged
A painting, a new life
Wet dry across the world, O-Ho!

Every time a distinct shape mark
Who cares how long it takes—desire!

CANDY HAND

TOOTHSOME OBSCURITIES

CANDY HAND
Sugar Baby

who knows why kind of fun

At Duxbury Point, a few thousand feet from here
The wind blows heavy 35 miles per hour all night long
Big lights at the postoffice illuminate Brighton Avenue
The raccoons can see to get across

                              •

As I pass through the dark dining room
I perceive that each chair is occupied by dwarf-
                ghoul-corpse
(Yammering. Decomposing. Power.)

                              •

Blithering dead leaves along the ground
Crooked sunlight falling smoke black wind
Electric power failure woke me up, I broke
The kitchen clock. Franco & Judy hungry in Zurich.

30:xii:68—Bolinas—11:xi:69—Kyoto

Birthday Poem,

In Advance of the Occasion of My Next One (If Any) 1967.

•

"Who, pray, of himself ever seeks out and bids a stranger from abroad, unless it be one of those that are masters of some public craft, a prophet, or a healer of ills, or a builder, aye, or a divine minstrel who gives delight with his song? For these men are bidden all over the boundless earth."

Odyssey XVII, 382–386 (A. T. Murray, Tr.)

•

"The Scholiast (n. 2 Lactantius Placidus, *Commentarius in Stattii Thebaida*, ed. R. Jahnke (Leipzig, 1898), X, no. 793) refers to a Gaulish custom of selling their lives for money, and, after a year of feasting, allowing themselves to be stoned to death by the populace."

Nora K. Chadwick: *The Druids*
(Cardiff, University of Wales Press: 1966)

•

Thank God, I don't have to write a poem
All those primulas raving potted hybrids
Mossy brim of brick fish pond

Only the biggest yellow-flowering one
Saves this day from death's vagrom fingers gloom & sad

Thank God none of those who read my poems don't see me
Don't realize I'm crazy, what book shall I carry with me
Lonesome for my own handwriting

A year among strangers, the Japanese all are mad
They look at me, can't forgive me for being funny-looking

That one's eating buttered toast in a way I never saw
      anybody eat anything
Rearranging his hair between whiles, daubing it
      with his hanky,

He turns to watch the primulas and back to his toast
            in the most decorative possible manner
What would he say if he got the chance he keeps
            talking to himself all the time, some
            kind of professor
And a buddhist, he bowed to the toast before eating it

I go and visit Honen Shonin vision stone and operatic
                pine tree Mt Yoshida
Up the hill through the graveyard we die into stone
Manjusri's pagoda lion laugh dim wise face not visible
But inside the back door of Manjusri's house there is
Sakyamuni! Lump skull pokes up through fringy hair
            also needs a shave

Costume all fine colors flaking and curling away
Neither smiling nor sad he watches the wooden doors

In front of Shinyodo baby soup yells and wiggles in the stone catch basin
And so up the last ridge to hilltop Shinto shrine
Break across and down to deer-pen cryptomeria courtyard
Octagonal god-house
Parents and children bow

What did I see then? What did I remember? That it was lost,
Now it is gone. I could see myself writing and coffee
I invoke Rodin's head of Balzac
Photo-engraving in Biedermeier frame:
            St Honoré aidez-moi!
(Honorius Bishop of Montmartre? Honorius: 4 popes,
            "*. . . empereur d'occident de 395 à 423 un des plus
            misérables souverains de la décadence*"
Balzac: "*. . . brillant et très fécond . . . . malgré certaines
            imperfections de style et la minutie de quelques de-
            scriptions . . .*")
                St Honoré preserve us against black coffee
                These Japanese knickknacks & from writing ourselves

To death instead of dope, syphilis, the madhouse, jail,
Suicide

The world is wicked by definition; my job is to stay aware of it
Bundles of cut weed carrying on
Without a world without an answer
Mukade put their heads in a ring a furry poison star

Bite through paper-thin shell of one segment of his back (giant
        mukade)
There's a kind of orange tree growing and green grass
Hesperides? I freezing, wrap myself and all my clothes in tired
        surplus Army mummy bag.
I think of all the words I've written.
What a funny thing to do. And who was he, that writer?

Shimogamo Bridge somebody made young stone corrals
        middle of the Kamo River
Double-motion projection of streetcar (moving water moving along
        steel tracks the moving bridge)
Sunset behind Mt Atago of a kind which causes religious conversions
        bad poetry, suicides
Honen Shonin understood that it was Buddha Land Purple Cloud
        Express

Upstairs where the action is all the quality folks
I sit downstairs under the loudspeaker (Peter Paul & Mary)
Spill bright barlight splash ice breaking
You just imagine that the Quality don't wear pointed shoes
Downstairs we got gangsters, too,
Neckties and hair. Hawaiian steel guitars
Café de Jeunesse I celebrate my middle age

        B E I N G,

Madam, I thank you for being what I am
Illegal, shapeless and mistaken

Because you have let me know it and kept quiet
Don't press charges, prepared your next lesson
Impersonally committed
How do I know where I'm at without you?

> "The Sumerian astronomers worked the rhythm out into
> a Saros, a useful period of 6,585-1/2 days. This was based
> on the distances of time between recurrent eclipses of
> both sun and moon, and it is accurate to one day in 1,800
> years."
>> C. A. Burland: *The Magical Arts, A Short History*
>> (Arthur Baker Ltd., 20 New Bond Street, London W.1)

A MAXIM:

> Always volunteer; never perform. This is benevolence.
> This is correction of the Will. Ted Williams went and
> spit on the grass.

Go now and write properly. Black shiny varnish. Was the paper
greasy. Paper or whatever non-operational as of Saturday 22:iv:
67 Mertis's water pump broke down there was nothing to Hell
with it let's go to the movies a perennial problem, Brian says so

> Inside the winter you'll find the loser
> Inside the winner you will find the string
> Playing music will clarify the mind
> Ask me another, I'll tell you again

"TOMORROW NIGHT I WILL BREAK DOWN THE DOOR"

> Inside the autumn find the singer
> Beside the summer lies the harp and the water falls
> Permanently
>> between two stars
>>> The Golden Stairs

Or step out of hot smoky Greyhound bus (car?) from California into
cold mountain air back home in Oregon rank and green smell of moss

194

ferns duff and bracken. Quite near the tavern store bus-stop wood-shed there's fresh sawed and split cedar and fir: orange sticky sugar. Slashpile smoke across highway, logged-over lot next to 1/2-finished two-story house with dormer windows flapping black tarpaper roof and walls out there somewhere between Oakridge and Chemult I always hate to leave this ugly place, living here is endless labour,

>"grub out stumps, fix up the place so the little woman don't complain too much of the time, TV set and cable service from Eugene electric drive antenna rig, well with electric pump, all-electric kitchen and laundry stuff, cow for the kids, six or eight hens, run chainsaw for Pope & Talbot, little carpentering, drive cat, little rigging, half-ass mechanic, Weyerhauser beef, my brother-in-law got a gyppo outfit over the mountain"

Summer
   crumbles August
lightning shatters
   temporarily the dead air
thick breakaway
   brilliant wind, new sky
Release from hot wooly I sail
   soar upwards in unlimited sweeps and swings
   out of sight again
Turn flying rainstorm
   upside
   down
Earth sprays water upwards
Lightning bursts from ground to cloud (the heat's broke lid)
new air coldest remote spaces
   crashes in

Charles Olson appears to me in a dream to denounce Irwin Panofsky
What I have to do is practise music. Spending money isn't the answer.
Dope is only temporary. Magic is more useful and exact.

Homer says if it weren't for death all of us would babble endlessly,
  "Tithonus shut in behind the shiny doors"

And the canons in *The Art of Fugue* and in *The Musical Offering* . . .

I wouldn't allow myself to buy one of those things because
I couldn't remember its Japanese name and yesterday
I disgraced myself at the market, calling an onion "egg"
My grandfather's name was Charles. Confucius has warned us all
       "KEEP NAMES AND WORDS *STRAIGHT!*"

Overcoming insuperable obstacles I attain Sukhavati Land
Field of Chinese bell-flowers Hoshun In, waterlilies don't quite bloom
      around the corner
On this side of the temple a meadow in the Sierra,
Lilypond and moon-viewing tower a surprise around the corner
Door painting of storks, the small, never-mentioned stone garden,
Elegance all thrown away chinchilla coat drug along by one sleeve

Leads (*via* Hollywood) into strange Kyoto present memory
Flying every day for many months early morning B-17
      (TOMORROW?)
My name was Dumbo then, leather skin high-altitude elephant,
      dangling oxygen trunk
      (TOMORROW EARLY)
pink hydraulic hairoil fluid
Ethyl-ester perfume airplane fuel for cigaret lighter
Oxygen for hangover
      (A HOME IN THE ARMY)
Fall asleep reading Whitman Civil War riding in the greenhouse
      high above the Chocolate Mountains
All one short enormous life
      how possible went?
Shall I be late tomorrow?
      (EARLY. SEVEN DAYS A WEEK.)
      with Jeanette MacDonald's husband
      (SMILIN' THROUGH)
      for an airplane driver
How did I ever get here? Enormous possibilities all miscarried
Long impossible early life
      bestowed   becalmed   bedizened

Lovely desert mornings early every day
Mornings early every flying day twenty-three years ago

SUNDAY PICK UP NEW SYKO SHEET IN FLIGHT SHACK

Hot weather demons box me in
I drum and trumpet a shower of rain
Remember to be careful with magic
Try for money next time. Jewels & money.
The demons are in the pay of IRS and the Treasury Department
Where's my bear suit?

> ". . . by that time we were all going to pieces," Joan
> Christophel used to say, "Naturally there was nothing
> we could do."

Crumbling.

temporarily; everything changed after all—
I heard Eric Dolphy's record, "Out to Lunch"

Hunting lotuses three Sundays
> 1. Sunday a bud and several big leaves. The Chinese mu-
> seum (Fujii Yurinkan) shut. Walk through soft willow hair.
> 2. Sunday cost ¥100, found big leaves. The Victoria lily had
> been blooming; enormous rotting cabbage blossom, starry
> nenuphars, cacti and orchids. 3. Sunday found strawberry
> ice, parts of Higashi Honganji moat full of big leaves and
> buds, one giant blowsy pink LOTUS flopping in the wind—
> quite by accident I find carved lintel of buck and doe from
> Gary's poem

> > Father Wieger says that in *Erh-Ya Encyclopedia* (11th Cen-
> > tury B.C.?) "The things of this world were distributed
> > under sixteen sections: kindred, houses, utensils, music,
> > heaven, earth, mounds, hills, waters, plants, trees, in-
> > sects, fishes, birds, wild & domestic animals."

As the night progresses the heat
Seems to increase the politics of summer
The electric fan drags a sheet of heavy silk across my skin
Mahler, Strauss, Bruckner compose this weather
Mozart brings no relief, my lechery increases
And sleep's heavy dopey sponge-rubber hammer
Waits to press me down again at any moment
The struggle for socialist realism cannot be relaxed a single second
My hands their thick veins lined with greasy fat sweated from the
Flesh of workers! Why did I let General Sarnoff do it to me
RCA and all! Arthur Godfrey!
All power to the ghosts of Henry George and Havelock Ellis!
Down with the Menshevik PTA!
While I sit here full moon electric fan Rachmaninoff
I'm also shut up in a small round wooden tub
Lid tied on with red string, miaowing
How can I work all rotted with silliness and war?
What would come out if I cut the string later tonight when nobody's
        looking?
DEMONS   HUNGRY GHOSTS   HELL WORLDS
Big as life I murdering I
No wonder I feel nasty inside.

Hope's bare shoulder when the soap is gone,
That was Lewy in this morning's dream of huge bare dusty
Coffeeshop and bar where he sits in window
Very young sad and dark hair girl with him,
"The European models have wrecked us all; they spit blood in my cunt!"

The girl says she feels particularly bad about it,
If she has been eating peacock the night before.
Lewy is angry and sad. The girl is tragic and tough.
Slide out of dream and weep on Hope's bare shoulder when
The soap is gone. A dream of drinking wine.

Autumn comes now triumph chrysanthemum harvest
Moon burnished persimmon plumed suzuki grass

The spirit perishes when the season turns.
Exhausted by summer, the autumn finds me sick as March
And winter just past. What do I see a hundred fish
Survived seventy miles of poisoned water, three million fishermen
Flash silver bug feed flip.

What do I see fish seller grabs a fly out of the air
Noplace to wipe his fingers

What do I see big fat boy baby in his pram
Examines a great lotus root

What do I see the sky is overcast for autumn full moon
Invisible *mochi* rabbit mortar
Silent apparition waves peacock feather:

"E M E R A L D S"

and slowly vanishes

A small fat young dog very sick
Tied by too short rope around its neck to the bottom rung of a ladder
Orange plastic garbage can beside it, upside down,
                 perfectly clean

Sporting goods clerk sits on metal folding chair behind
The counter stroking the front of his pants he smiles
The other boy sits in front of a big mirror combing his hair
                 some new exciting way
Neither attends the TV which offers them unlimited wealth,
Eternal life, unchanging beauty, new sex potency, endless love

Gently. Double Ten 1967. Gently.
                 but nothing can be done so slowly
Except that balloon which rises higher into thinner atmospheres
All the gas within its delicate rubber hide slowly pushed the mem-
                 brane beyond the breaking point

Rupture occurs gently as a gum boil, an ulcerated molar. . . .
Immediately but measurable: the second of time being
Marvelously divisible by electronic means
Blast the gas disperses its molecules glide ever upwards
Among the heavier ones of the air, gas never completely in control
Anyway—lots of it marching carelessly out between fat
Resilient rubber chains

       Dr Sun Yat Sen proclaimed a new life
It lasted thirty years; it was old at twenty
      S P O I L T
the idea of a revolution, an universal suffrage, a parliament
Free total education Roman alphabet gentle progress towards
The Realization of the Human Potential &c &c
Now the latest medicine show, newest suckerbait
New Model Shears to fleece the rubes in Minnesota Viet Nam
What color is the government, red or white?
It is gold, no matter what motto whose face is minted on it
Gold on loan to certain politicians under certain extremely
Harsh and clear terms of restriction and interest
Blubber hooks attached to rubber chains
Anchored in the bank where the gold belongs to a very few men
Who like it very much

     The weather grows colder now but the leaves
     Have scarcely begun to turn color
     Dusty and wrinkled they hang on, permanently glued
     To the trees, absolutely insured against damage
     Caused by possible falling. October is almost half gone;
     The leaves aren't worried, the sun shines
     Although the nights are almost cold the leaves will stay
     Today. They won't fall tonight, either—

     Nevertheless in the morning one or three lie
         ACCIDENTALLY
           on the ground
     Nobody saw them fall, the dusty green ones on the tree

Flap quite carelessly in the breeze, who ever heard of
                    November?

Who's got the money and what are they buying with it
Greece a brand new fascist government
South Korea some kind of ok stable government
Guatemala safe in the hands of reliable cardinals and archbishops
Who knows about Viet Nam?
            The mystery is fun up to the point where it's used
            for outright bilking and bamboozling the beholder,
            killing his children, distracting him while
            the government extracts his blood,

                "A L B I O N, A W A K E!", *et cetera*

In America we have everything, we say "God is dead"
Hoping to shock Chairman Mao (the bank is neither frightened
                    nor surprised)
The Giant in Chains, the toughy safely entombed beneath Mt Etna,
The certified corpse of Jesus all carefully sealed in heavy guarded tomb
Safely put away—the embarrassment he caused! The unseemly,
Untimely, politically naive impractical theorist suppressed at last
Finally, completely, once and for all,

            but the season UNACCOUNTABLY changes, the leaves
            all brilliantly fall, thousands at a time,
            Yellow red stripey and tawny splotchy crackling
            vegetable brocade foam around my ankles
            (new cold makes them ache) the sun blares through
            naked branches
            wind blasted smoke of burning leaves dead twigs fallen
            bark
            swirls the black thick plume at the mountain peak
            the great solid boulder tomb door
            throbs like a drum the sky
                    shatters,

Now all rationalized into a whole different notation, meaning
                  and purpose.
The lady in the gold hat dances because the *tsuzumi* orange silk
Ropes loosen drum tone glides, his foot shifts
Balances on its heel. Drum thump: sky-pointing toe
Switches exactly to the right and stops a while,
No more music or dance, only animal breathing harsh
Half stifled behind lacquer mask whose outside shows
Calm silent gentle sadness
                  the whole figure, mask wig golden hat brocade clothes
white underwear and *tabi* all means something else

the drum says P L O K the toes of that foot
Point straight up again.
The figure is monumentally present, no time has passed
Only that furious hospital death-ward breath
Monstrous, apart, static, tense, rooted,

                  P   L   O   K
drum foot moves back lifts high off the floor as if to stomp
Comes down silently as the drum PLOK again
The drummer screams a single word the dancer performs a total
                  C O N T R A C T I O N
takes a few steps in a circle
Great green brocade bell (represents a couple tons of bronze casting)
lowers itself another two feet from the ceiling the drum
P L O K the lady's foot moves and stops, a new stop-motion cycle
Commences, varied now by a few short steps, then
the old pattern repeated, one drum-controlled movement at a time
Each motion followed by unendurable stillness and silence
And this time turning in a circle the lady repeats one word five times
And stop when the drum   PLOK
                  he holds her fan out away from her body
                        the angle carefully prescribed
                                    the smell of burning leaves the

smell of shaving-soap morning cigaret burning on the ledge
below the bathroom mirror goose pimple skin of Rome's Adam's
Apple turkey neck razor gently slow

PASSENGERS ON THE NATIONAL RAILWAY ARE KINDLY
REQUESTED TO REFRAIN FROM READING LITERATURE
CRITICIZING THE GOVERNMENT WHILE TRAVELING
THANK YOU

All I've got to say is, I've had my time.
If you aren't smart enough to have, get
Drop your own I can't cry for you any more
Dear friends, dear Government, dear Policemen
I am no longer interested in your ideas, your laws, your prejudices

Take a hoop and roll it

I laugh at you; I die and live continually
Imagining I care for you, you care for me

Lies & fraud

Nothing's genuine except imagination who creates
Whether we will or no: for fun
For boredom. For nothing.
I chose to appear in this place, to come to your party
I do it on purpose, over and over again
I hate parties, I always have a good time
And it always takes hours for me to recover my sanity
I go there to reassure you that the world is impractical
Magic and lunacy, poetry spells and music.

I don't even realize you don't understand that you don't need
The help that I imagine you need I imagine I bring

Imagining I (but that is only you:
All of us projections overlapping real transparent scene)

I must act right, I must intend right even when there's
No such thing as I or right I must choose correctly
Keep these muscles practising, always hit the right key
I can read the score perfectly well,
Nerves and coordination perfectly fine
Only a temporary case of mistaken identity
Claude Raines. Bette Davis. Herbert Marshall. Monty Woolley.
George Sanders. Edith Sitwell. Lionel Barrymore. Ethel Barrymore.

        moss carpet veil of tiny fallen maple leaves
      William Morris claustrophobia tapestry
Fragments of maple flowers unicameral legislatures
Tragic bimetalism. Oranges. Bergamot. Bigarade.
Bigarré .... *"qui a des couleurs ou des dessins variés ..."*
Burnt orange color of maple blossom
        metal bosom

QUIET

One surface of all I see is meditating Buddha Dai Nichi Nyorai
The reverse where I am now downtown Chicago five P.M. Monday
New York Philharmonic Orchestra Roger Shaw Choral & E. Power Biggs
        at the pipe organ

QUIET

and it is   COLD   in here
Mudra turns out to be childhood coldfinger crossfinger
"Doubletouch" daydream
Yantra in four dimensions discovered "double-fuck" fingerplay

How cleverly our teachers had it figured out
There were five senses five fingers.
Up until that time I knew that there were a great
Many more, senses whose names I don't remember
None the less real and present and functioning
Right now

joy fountains open earliest ether vision
brilliant light of 1929 penetrating
warmth brain face head grow glow like erecting
glans penis cobra's hood intense light and heat
orbicular ridge and supermaxillary sinuses
awakens me if it happens while I'm asleep

"Who been here since I been gone
Railroad worker with his gum-boots on"

Early in the morning what I see four hanging lamps
Two plate glass windows like department store plane-leaves
A stone wall with grey painted streamlined steel fence
Glued on top of it behind which is Kyoto University
Sometime under Imperial Patronage the stone wall has lots of
Green moss ten students and professors a cook a dishwasher
A waiter a potted palm a coal-oil heating stove
The coffee and croissants are a long time getting here
Streetcar shine bicycle handlebars

The Frog Child has a new brother
How's his insect taboo?
A green hole in the distance
Green diamond, beryl, emerald.
Professors and students now appear in
Brilliant feathers, plumes, gems, enamels
(Black palm fronds)
Each one is different. What is it they are eating.
Word word word word word click.

N.B., that St Augustine's pears were green;
John XXIII's were mildewed. (See
Vespasiano's *Life of Lionardo d' Arezzo*)

Two ancient tiny black-wadded-silk kimono ladies
One still a beauty, the other even older
Pure toothless benevolence quite strongly arose and

Crossed the aisle in the streetcar
To say something to the man sitting next to me,
Put something in his hand—money? Ticket?
Next she turned to me, gave me three big crystals
Pure rock candy. I thanked her and she sat down again
Beaming love and joy across the centuries
Right through the center of the language culture barrier

I hear the horns of elfland honking as I lean
As I lean out these magic Japanesey casements all forlorn
The bell

      I wrote the tune they're playing.
        The mermaids are singing my song
          It all sounds better than anyone could imagine

Vain shadows, I used to flee your mocks and fleers
Now the paint has flaked and crumbled from your shoddy veils
Adieu! Get them to a laundry, go . . .
      ("LAUNDERY," tri-syllabic)
And to those admirers of my work who find me an unpleasant man
Remember I am a harvested field
Winter orchard beehive
And to all my friends a secret unheard message:
      I'm always afraid you'll find out I love you
      Then you'll hate me. How much does this matter, anymore?

      Two zeroes is one hundred.
      Black to move and win.

Awake or asleep I live by the light of a hollow pearl

Kyoto—San Francisco—Kyoto 1967–1969

Excerpts from "Scenes of Life at the Capital"

Today I started late and quit early
And accomplished everything, but the next day was
Marred by fits of rage, mental confusion
Lapses of memory. Olson dead in New York
Jack dead in Florida. Today I am going to take more:
Smoked some and ate some
      OM.   AH.   HUM.
          in five sacred colors
I woke up a couple of times during the night
High with lights and music behind the eyes
This morning I am cured and know who and where I'm at

Why should I go to Europe to look at
Several million nervous white folks
My very own relatives there they are
Totally uncivilized, fingering and puzzling over
The ruins of Western Civilization
I feel closer to that culture which our ancestors
Destroyed . . . megalithic builders initiated in mushroom
Mysteries at Crete, Eleusis, New Grange

In this capital we also fumble with ruins of high culture
But feelings of antique propriety keep heavy sway
Over family, marriage, feudal obligations to a chief
The life of the Capital goes by in tight pants
Or on horseback brilliant silk *hakama*
Brocade *karaginu* gleaming lacquer hat

Summer's dead leaves philaudering into dusty moss
Like melting Dracula.
      (PHILAUDERING. *Mot imaginaire de l'auteur.*)
The soul extractors are here.

Edgar W. Tomczyk of Lima, Ohio, will now attempt
To drive a D-8 Cat through
Two inches of boiling water from which he will escape
Absolutely unharmed!
          (oops.)
Rupert Scanlon of Great Falls, Montana will now . . .

The world (and I)
Barge past the sun
Glass on stove's fuel-gauge reflects
The sun onto north wall twenty feet away
The passage of Time, the zooming of the earth
Can be witnessed as a disc of light
Sliding over dots of mud plaster sand
Other goop embedded in the surface

Daitokuji celebration day still echoes in my head
Sound of manhole-cover falling flat on stone floor
The rainy maples at Koto-In
Last night wild boar for supper
Shakuhachi music over snowy torrent
BOTAN NABE, Peony Cassoulet
So far north of the Capital the road is only paved
When it becomes (five seconds) mountain village mainstreet
among *sugi* trees ordinary dirt in the canyons
But the people speak *Kyoto-ben.*
BOTAN garden of Daitokuji monastery
Manhole-cover clang and crash
Big pair of cymbals, thin brass with center bowl
Broad-rim soup dishes B L A S H!
Everybody dolled up in brocade bib and tucker
Chinese canal-boat shoes, Nootka shaman hats
To exceed wisdom and ignorance escape skull chain
(Juzu beads I saw today each bead a white head-bone
Apparently impossible although there's enough space
Between bone crystals to drive a truck through)

There's not an owl in the world who thinks or knows
"I am an owl." Not one who knows there's a man called
Slotkin who knows more about owls and the owl trade
Than any owl. I wonder though,
Can Professor-Doktor Slotkin eat mice and fly.

Kyoto 6 P.M. News:
Somebody left a pistol in a raincoat in a taxi on
Higashiyama (Eastern Mountain) Road

New York Buddha Law:
All sentient beings will be brought
To complete final perfect enlightenment
If you will write a letter to *The New York Times*
Condemning Ignorance, Desire and Attachment.

Almost all Americans aged 4 to 100
Have the spiritual natures of Chicago policemen.
Scratch an American and find a cop. There is no
Generation gap.

I sit in the north room
Look out across the floor into the garden
12$^1/_2$ tatami mats the pleasure of contemplating them
They are beautiful and they aren't mine.
Present appearance of quiet neutral emptiness
Books, music, pictures, letters, jewels, machines
Buddha statues and other junk all hidden away
As if inside my head (think of the closets
As memory banks) Wooden ceilings pale orange
Floors the color of wheat straw, light-grey paper
Colored mountains near the bottom cover the fusuma
That divide rooms hide closets. Glass and white paper
Shoji screens two garden ends of the house north and south

Heavy floral designs of Michoacan
(Have you ever considered going THERE to live)

O flowers more lovely than wine
Adonis and/or Dionysus . . .
". . . only one note and it a flat one . . ."
"Only a rose
For you." (That was a long time ago.)
              (unique abyss)
              "I'll go along
              With a smile & a song
              For anyone . . ." all this was
Copyrighted maybe 1911 "ONLY A ROSE FOR YOU!"
So long ago I was a prisoner still and other people
Made everything happen good bad & indifferent
              "Control yourself!" they said
To survive continuous neural bombardment
Meningeal bubbles twenty years after—
Now I make things happen
These thin brass domes and birds of ice
Cheap fruity cries pop
There's your tricycle (from Jimmy Broughton's movie,
Mother's Day)
              tricycle from the Isle of Man
Three legs running
"The Shinto emblem showing three comma-shaped figures
in a whirl symbolizes the triad of the dynamic movements
of *musubi* . . ."—Jean Herbert

Athenian abyss   Tarquin Old Stairs   off the steep
edge of town   Delphi something else
          a friend writes from Eleusis: "nothing here
          but a vacant lot . . . factories in the distance"

    "Those caves of ice"

                 * * *

Minestrone
For all sentient beings

get me out of here! Bail me
out of the WORD OCEAN

"I wish to God
I never see your face
Nor heard your lion tongue"

And so knocked over my drink
I now have a pantsfull of cold sweet coffee
Hop up out of the way and white shirt all stained
On account of G. M. Hopkins:
"What do then? how meet beauty? Merely meet it; own,
Home at heart, heaven's sweet gift; then leave, let that alone.
Yea, wish that though, wish all, God's better beauty, grace."

Whatever any of that means (TO WHAT SERVES MORTAL BEAUTY?)
I am suddenly spastic brainless
Flailing arms and feet
Complete total mess. Rush home. Underwear
Hair and wristwatch and all pockets
Full of coffee syrup, take a bath to get rid of it
Before the ants can find me

Poor Hopkins imagined he had it completely under control
Set framed and crystallized
It all explodes iced coffee in ten directions,
Three worlds. He had to be a priest
Poetry was some other trip forced on him
Squirting out every nozzle, pore and orifice

I must have been reaching for my notebook
With both hands and several more
I wanted to copy that message here
Some arm and fingers held the Hopkins book

Yet other hands reaching for pen—did I yell,
I wonder—which of these hands arms elbows
Knocked the glass *towards* me?
                    coffee and sugar leaping in
                    capillaries of my brain
Coffee or sleep thick and sweet
Heavy chocolate hours of morning
Deliberately. And now 10:30 A.M. washed and broken away
From books and music I sit with my feet melting
In bright invisible mountain water that lies above
Brown chocolate mud and fir needles and little sticks
Two inches or twenty feet below—impossible to judge
Because of stillness and clarity of water
Smooth and heavy as cloth of cold
Black transparent stream,
                    anyway I thought that was the reason

SWAMI VIVEKANANDA: ". . . Like an insane person I ran out of our
                     house. He asked me, 'What do you want?' I
                     replied, I want to remain immersed in
                     samadhi. He said: 'What a small mind you
                     have! Go beyond samadhi! Samadhi is a
                     very trifling thing.' "

In the capital the commonest materials—
mud, plain paper, a couple boards and a bush and a rock,
A handful of straw—stuff we think of as worthless
Throw it away, certainly not to use for building a house
But set here in proportion, in specific spatial relation
An order of decorum and respect for themselves
Out of nothing at all, a house and garden
That can't last more than ten minutes
Very quietly stays forever

Here at the edge of town people visit me
As they used to hike up Sauk Mountain
Or to the Sourdough Lookout. They sidle up
And say, "Ain't you kind of lonely

Up here all alone?" I have to lie and say
"Sometimes," because they look injured & rejected
If I say "No." The truth is that living
In remote and foreign places takes a lot of
Work, every day, no time to feel sad and friendless

The neighborhood barber watches my hair walk by
Jealously. So much for
The Law of Karma.

Where is Los Angeles? Where IS Los Angeles
In among the minnie-bombs & maxi-toons
Cloud, altocumulus, as appears above islands
Far at sea.
O California lardy-dar

What is California, nothing but South Alaska
        "See how CANADA comes me cranking in
        And cuts me from the best of all my land
        A huge half-moon, a monstrous cantle out . . ."
                                Northern Chile
I didn't know what I was getting into
Until it was too late and now I am a   F R E A K !
            O California!
    A   G R E A T   B I G   F R E A K
                (ugh!)

almost white granite with little stars
Juniper trees in high California
Recollected at a great distance
Everyplace else forgot
Thinking "Moon still important at
The capital" and "L'AIDE-MEMOIRE DE LA VRAIE LOI"

An awfully large number of us
Had our heads bent with nowhere theories
Presented in beguiling books
Marx and Lenin, Freud and Jung, Churchill and Lord Keynes

Kafka and Kierkegaard,
In spite of or on account of which
Becoming cannon-fodder for sadist politicians
Patients of expensive quacks. How come.

> "In short, he bid me goe to the Fountain head,
> and read Aristotle, Cicero, Avicenna, and did call
> the Neoteriques shift-breeches."
> —Aubrey's *Life of Wm. Harvey*

I suspect you can be as nutty with a head full
Of Greek and Latin, but maybe less easily imposed upon
And perhaps a little less dangerous?

Anthony à Wood, *Life & Times:* "In this month [*May*] was
to be seen at the Fleur de luce [*inn at Oxford*]
a brasen head that would speak and answer."

Neighbor's new iron gate sound
Bones of my right arm and elbow.

Always. America. Always a line of people
Ten or fifteen of them, all very smart
Waiting at the madhouse door to their parents' bedroom
Walking in their sleep—what time is it.
What does "dromedary" actually mean.
Cancel my subscription to TRAK Service.

Banana trees now at their best.
But the most exciting green is rice in the paddy
Just beginning to produce ears of grain
Middle of August, shimmering subliminal green waves
And secret power-vibes
Maybe high quality emeralds can do
A similar job? However, the rice is alive
To be eaten later or brewed into *sake*
And so transports us out of Oregon skull

The sea's defective music as a passing bull
Suborns eleven
I can tell.

"AWAY, THOU FONDLING MOTLEY HUMOURIST!"

An overdose of America
Money and too many decibels

        Miss Janice climb up
        On a white snow horse
        Never climb down any more

O Sunflower, mouldy with grime, &c
Waste and want. Sung flower?

An overdose of pure London
Took Jimi Hendrix away,

    ". . . rueful again the piteous bagpipe went
    O bag-pipe thou didst steal my heart away"
        ("Fled music is the sweetest
        My Fair Lady")
"Of late two dainties were before me plac'd"

John Keats also lost

        "that's going to be him, see, how
        Monkey Face slips down over Great Seal
        Eyes and proliferation of curves
        From working too fast before the epipyroxylin
        Cools"

        Yukio MISHIMA, novelist, playwright, actor,
        Suicide by elegant Japanese tradition

Produces the effect of an infinite territory
What?

With only one possible neighboring color
What? Monads?

No, there's, no, no, not nomads, no, no
That idea was discredited, can't work, David Hume
What about volvox colonies
Universe of spheres containing spheres
All individual, all neighbors with independent spheres
Inside, so beautifully Buchsbaum
Never mourned, no eyes, what

FERN

the effect of uninterrupted acceleration (how-
ever familiar the track) certain contact-plates
prepare trees light up animals move and sing
laugh in the dark

EMERALDS

* * *

I drink bad expensive Italian wine
Beside the Kamo River. They say
You've taken a new lover. Passengers
On Sanjo Bridge Hieizan profile
Now all marvelously smudged by pen of hispid friend
Bottled somewhere near Florence, I expect
All the customers in here will rise and applaud
When I leave this place. They have been profoundly
Edified by the spectacle of a certified FOREIGNER
Gobbling up a pizza with his fingers
Drinking a bottle of wine without falling off his chair
A scene of life at the capital

I haven't been drunk for a long time
Reminds me of you, before we all

Became dope-friends. When was your last trip,
I went cuckoo on LSD the 30th of April

There's already been a great deal said about wine
And I'm reading the faggoty part of *The Anthology*
Thinking of you instead of naked boys
Curious elision. I've drunk 0.475 liter of "chianti"
Much too fast. Antinori. (Antenor was a mythological
What did he do?)

Hieizan sadder and smaller than Mt Koya
But still a mountain in several senses
Even though they drive buses to it
The buses go home at night; the trees take over
You can step out of temples into rhododendron flowers
                    ruins
Path which Mas Kodani followed seven days in rain
Priest robes, shaman hat, straw sandals too small,
Would wild monkeys attack him? Reciting HANNYA SHINGYO
Wherever stone marker on the trail shows where temple was

What was I saying. Talking to you.
A slow green train leaves for Uji
A slow green train arrives from Osaka
Immediately departs. I just realized that all I've said
For the past ten years was addressed to you
Simple and flat as that.

Kite! not the toy, a living bird
Sails above Kamogawa, that same Goddess
In worldly form dips and swings
Far below a northbound airplane
"KEE-REE!"
                "The hawk flies up to heaven"

I have to write this at home with a new pen
I pitched the other into the Kamo
The moment it lifted from writing "—REE!"

To the complete consternation and horror
Of the other guests

> Now this Antenor has a curious history.
> Brother-in-law to Priam, King of Troy,
> he betrayed the Palladium to the Greeks
> that they might capture the Capitol. He
> escaped with his family to found New Troy
> in Italy (Venice or Padua?) the father of
> the prophet, Laocoön. Pious Aeneas founded
> a second Troy at Rome. Noble Brutus founded
> Troynovaunt, *alias* London, capital of the world?

"It is said in the Book of Poetry, 'The hawk flies up
to heaven; the fishes leap in the deep.' "

Horror & chagrin of other patrons
Who carefully preserve their papers, ink and brushes and ink-
Stones in elegant lacquer boxes.
Writing is a serious action presided over by a god,
Tenjin-O-Mi-Kami-Samma, at the Kitano Shrine

All these worlds change faster than I can tell you
I have this reading & writing habit which I cultivate
Excessively, perhaps, little time for anything else
Although it's fun to ride the Osaka zipper
Forty-eight minutes for 65 miles
Fast asleep to Yodoyabashi branch Bank of America

Sound asleep we leave the capital rainy night
(Boats which children might have made from apple boxes)
Passengers remaining awake rattle their beads
Call on Amida Buddha and Kwannon to save them

Under the cushions and the *goza* matting
I feel the planks bulge as they slide
Snail foot over boulders and rocks

Far in the middle of the river
Safe and dry sound asleep left Sōō Temple, Yamazaki Bridge
At sundown. Early morning waken to shouts
Boatswarm harbor of Naniwa
Thanks to Gods of Sumiyoshi!

                          *   *   *

Japan is a civilization based upon
An inarticulate response to cherry blossoms.
So much for Western Civilization.
"Mr. Franklin, is it a setting or a rising sun?"
Try to be serious. Try to get to Toji tomorrow.
Try to remember that I accidentally found
Birthplace of Shinran Shonin when I visited Hokaiji
Magnolias and cherries at Daigoji.
Unprecedented splendor.

Look into the abyss and enjoy the view.
All we see is light; all we don't see
Is dark. We know lots of other things
With other senses. Various kinds of new green weeds
Pop up through white gravel

Chicago, Federal Court, *USA* vs *Dellinger et al. #69 Crim.* 180:
Mr KUNSTLER: "The whole issue in this case is language,
                      what is meant by . . ."

Mr Thomas HAYDEN, a Defendant: "We were invented."

Poetry, American. (see under *American Poetry*)
In the U.S.A. "Calliope" is a steam piano.
Nobody ever figured out that Sir Gawain's Green Knight
Was a crocodile (*pace* Yvor Winters)

Revisit Kitano plum blossoms
Pink ones have strong perfume.

Big tree in front of central sanctuary
(*Gongen-Zukuri* architecture, Sugawara Michizane
Was incarnation [*gongen*] of this Deity who presides
Over plum blossoms and calligraphy and scholarship)
So hollow and full of holes it scarcely exists at all
But blossoms immensely before scarlet fence
Intricate wooden gables
Another all propped up with poles and timbers
Part of it fixed with straw rope
Exploding white blossoms not only from twigs
And branches but from shattered trunk itself,
Old and ruined, all rotted and broken up
These plum trees function gorgeously
A few days every year
In a way nobody else does.

At the Capital 44–46 Showa
25 January

Many Colored Squares

Why decide in advance what to do. Eucalyptus trees their shiny
leaves and polished crows. The opera of. Hummingbirds. MOVE,
an optimum crow call and spider sparkle newly. Joe walks but
seldom touches the ground. Pause. Hammer. Pause. Wind. Crows.

What's in the oven. All the ingredients: quit opening the door if
you want Dinner to emerge in less than a geological epoch. Oh.
Busy. Hmmm.

Sniff.

Of something. The first fruits of man's disobedience was a
                                                    pomegranate
The invention of Winter and Ambition—The joyful desiring. Flat out.

KONK

Much better under lots of Monterey cypresses and immense blue-gum
and lemon-wood; trees in the distance in front of the ocean. Letch.

The disobedient mind is the fruit of inactivity swaying upon dishonest
boughs. The butcher's thumb lies weighty on the scales. Tumble.

Minor chords are not sad. The Pyramids are still a secret. Erasmus
Darwin: *The Botanic Garden.*

The explanation isn't the same as what happens. A recipe can produce
a particular result most of the time.

Carrie turned all the matches in the same direction. Love and Honor
conspire to discipline the Factory.

Come with me, Joe.

Now when Bill gets here we will leave. Quite seriously. Stop tittering.

Cut straight down the center it means twice as much. Free at last.
Or not. Hand lotion soothes my mind. Correspondence.

Scales uncolored in themselves produce a rainbow. Mountain seafoot
absolutely white? Iron curl. Start over. Start all over again. Your
feet are dirty on the bottom. I won't say "Immensely so."

Container for insensible fruit?

22:vi:71

"Up in Michigan"

Tough branch stems blue
Chicory flowers
Down flat leaves almost dandelion
Blue delicate five-tooth petal edge
Almost invisible thread hair center
Lots of Queen Anne's lace, Joel misquotes Williams,
"Wild carrot invades a whole field"
Big leaf trees where land floats outward
Glacier tundra peat prairie
The sun rises in the north

Allendale, Michigan, 13:vii:71

"Old Age Echoes"

Lately I've seen myself
As fat naked waddling baby
All alone in the yard
Bright flowers
Silver lawnmower blades
Big dog approaching (friendly?)
Berries
What are fears or dangers?

19:vii:71

The Letter to Thomas Clark 22:VII:71
from Bolinas where He Sat beside Me
to Help to Write It

Tom Clark
Waco, Texas

(crossed out. All our
addresses crossed out)

Dear Tom. Received your letter
& no mistake
about the address or the sender (name of
Angelica) but

you
look just the least bit changed.

Due to this minuscule point
and the fragility
of the ink,
And the wrong time of day all over town
It was not the phone.

but
(the fragility. . . .
of one's own neuromuscular mechanism
where that S W A M P)

Yours truly,
Dad.

"Horrible Incredible Lies": Keith Lampe Spontaneously

"THE NEXT WOMAN THAT COMES THROUGH HERE THAT I WAS FOND OF IN A REALLY NOBLE ROMAN LANDSCAPE WHERE LARGE FREEDOMS TO DO A NUMBER, *viz.* A DOUBLE MARRIAGE PERFORMED BY A.J. MUSTE THE EVENING I THINK HE GOT CERTIFIED LANGUAGE FOR GADFLY LEAFLETS IN 1967 MORE ASHTRAYS AS HAD BEEN SOUVENIRS HO CHI MINH HAD LAID ON HIM A COLUMN OF GREEN FLAME SHOT UP BEING THE SOUVENIR ASHTRAY MADE FROM A MAGNESIUM FRAGMENT WHICH HE PROBABLY DIED A HIERONYMOUS MISTAKE A PEOPLE APART FROM ANITA HOFFMAN PUTTING DOWN A PLAGUE ON BOTH YOUR INCREDIBLY DEIFIED HOUSES. NITA NEVER HAD A SAW AN EXPANSION BETWEEN THESE TWO THINGS WITHOUT EVER LOOKING.

"REALITY LOOKED AT HIM AND SMILED AND THAT VERY MINUTE WENT CLICK, NEURAL SPEED, A TOTAL DINOSAUR SCENE IN MONUMENT VALLEY SHE MET A SURFER DOWN AN OLD RIVERBED CRUNCHING THE GRAVEL WHICH SOUND ALLOWS HER ACCESS TO LIT-UP DINOSAURS THREE DAYS OF ISOLATED VERBALIZATION FOR A WHILE TO RECOVER BETTER WHEN THE STARS COME OUT."

3:viii:71

Imaginary Splendors

As I stand here I feel myself growing older and impatient
with you, this endless failing life won't reach you, too
short on one end, walk around upstairs and sing wreck my
nerves I'm going to bed I want out of this amusement park,
the holidays are over I must go back to work (if I could find
a job I couldn't stand it) the one person who doesn't need all this
explanation I want to talk to him is gone, probably dead and
what have I got to say

                                    and catch
myself again completely unaware of what's real around me here.
Imaginary jumps out of the closet plays my nerves and feelings
the sun trees flowers don't exist Imaginary grabs all my attention
sucks energy out my spinal column Imaginary debauchery all bankrupt
what becomes of all that circuitry the needles read OVERLOAD there's
a leak far below the waterline the pumps are burning out huge power
of ocean waves heavy radiation from sun all escaping headed for total
heaviness turned inside out anti-matter sox tube to other Universe

what about most delicate redwood needle shadows
heavy slow tops of eucalyptus
beaded fringe skirt of Texas Guinan
small Hieronymus Bosch California fuchsias

                    hummingbird a tremendous
                        D Y N A M O
                    no float or zap through the air
                    anti-gravity syrup in all those flowers?

Sun so powerful here
Giant lilies grow in the shade
        "When I say, 'JUMP, MR DEAD MAN,' you go!"

                                        7–10:viii:71

227

Public Opinions

Peter Warshall says that the slow loris moves approximately three feet per hour.

Donald R. Carpenter says, "I don't do ANY hot water numbers in the morning."

Allen Ginsberg, reading a ms poem handed to him by a friend, says, "AH, that's green armpit poetry."

Irving Oyle says: What did Chekov do but live in a small town where everybody said, "Some day I'll go to Moscow"?

What I say is that in every toke you could taste the cold slick throb of real DOPE: fine East India hemp.

                E A R T H Q U A K E
        DUCKY FAULT SLIP
        DUCKY FALSE LIP?
                "no effect on me, whatsoever."

12:viii:71

Monument Rescue Dim

Her mouth is empty
All the sky shines
Bird feet on the roof
Did the telephone ring

MAGNIFICENT

(a silence)
Dromedary
I keep hearing something else

You continue babbling on without making any sense at all why not
Neither of us attending as in a dream wherein everything important
Happens "offstage" somewhere just beyond the view of the sleeping eye

14:viii:71

The Turn

Walking along Elm Road
Handful of nasturtiums, butter, some kind of bread
75¢ the loaf no advertising included
Bread and air and a price tag wrapped in plastic
The dogs come out as usual to roar at me
I find myself screeching wildly in reply
Fed up with suppressing my rage and fear
I bellow and roar
The dogs are scared and their people scandalized
"What are you trying to do? HAY! What are you trying to do?"
I had nothing to tell them; I was talking to their dogs.

16:viii:71

Look   Look   Look

My eyes fondle carved metal and stone
Suck up jeweled faceted bronze nasturtium leaves and flowers
Feed and nourish strapped sense glued in bone marrow
We would rather swim, dance

Eyes glance and glide over polished surfaces
Lacquer gold yes I test it with my thumb
Solid
Impossible to believe that all I see is light
Reflected from images and ritual implements
Thunderbolt bell
Gleaming vajra

"Love in fantastic triumph sate . . ."

16:viii:71

"I Told Myself":
Bobbie Spontaneously

"I TOLD MYSELF THAT I WASN'T GOING TO GET HIGH TODAY:
AND I TOLD MYSELF THAT IF I *DID* GET HIGH
IT WASN'T GOING TO BE ON ACID—
BUT I THOUGHT TO MYSELF, WELL MAYBE
IF I JUST BROKE A LITTLE CORNER OFF IT
THERE'D STILL BE AN *AWFUL* LOT OF IT LEFT . . .
A CORNER OFF TODAY,"

16:viii:71

Growing and Changing

WHAMP WHAMP WHAMP
and squeal of skill-saw
I carelessly build a creepy future life

All things made new and completely wrong

Once too often
Made all new
Laid bare *"mon coeur*
mis à nu"
Our time is one two many
anew (*agneau*)
Desuetude

I guess you are somebody
I used to know
One that I knew
Then. Guess who.

Imagine living on Telegraph Hill
worrying

Imagine living anywhere
worrying
"Just
a-wearying
for you"

THIS MEANS YOU
(underlined in red)
Let me interest you unwearyingly
END OF SONG APPROACHING
ROUGH DETOUR AHEAD

KRANK

Perhaps you have often wondered why I have
so seldom written to you. I am put off by knowing
how busy you are and by the crowd of affairs which
presses for my attention almost every waking minute
(nevertheless many members of that crowd are mem-
ories of you and speculations about your present
activities, feelings and states of mind). I often
tell myself

(large comma)

. . . the idea of your thinking of me doesn't make much sense
either, on a day when I am properly organized and orientated, but I
am susceptible to quick changes of mood—
a drink of gin rearranges my mind right away
and I can see you frowning and moodily
thinking of me: a train of unsatisfactory pictures/thoughts
which annoy you and your annoyance reaches me instantly
and of course it is all completely absurd I am attending
to the boiling chicken and you are wondering "blue or
green? Where are the scissors. Did Peter buy tomatoes
again?" The integuments of reality great floating sticky
transparent films of regret and misplaced concern &
hankering,

A day. I can spend all kinds of time
Considering which word to set beside this one.
The life of art

I think I'm going to do just that
And washed all my shirts
Every plastic one
This is no different from any other day except for the memory
Of Saturn. Later all the gods churned the sea
To recover certain immortality a stolen woman
Make me turn my head and say
"What was that?", if you want me to like it.

Whom does one ask.
Who do you ask.

>   Whom does;
>   One asks.

Who do you ask
And your dreams reply
(very much like Henry James)
"There you are."

1–9:ix:71

and what. One must groan and stretch in order to break
any habit. The process of developing new muscles hurts.
Pain causes anger. I find myself quarrelling over nothing.
O! O! O!

Find twenty beautiful pages for Thomas Clark.
> ("Anything!", Joanne Kyger said. "I'd write anything
> that I could!")

Twenty things hitherto unincluded:
1. *Shakujo*
2. Copy of *The Wooden Fish*
3. Medal from Rokuhakudo
4. Piece of lapis lazuli, gift of J. Armstrong
5. Indian shrine, gift of J. Kyger
6. Blue Mexican glass pitcher
7. Three onyx eggs
8. Three cylindrical magnets
9. Tanka of Chenrezig, gift of Claude Dalenberg
10. Necklace of elephant bells
11. Drawing of P.W. by J-L. Kerouac
12. Blue tin trunk
13. Pebble of rutilated quartz carved into Daruma image
14. Two shakuhachi, and other Japanese instruments
15. Round fan, woven by the last Carib Indian in the West
    Indies, "Use it for setting hot things on," Anne Waldman
    when she gave it to me.
16. Japanese wristwatch
17. Crystal inkwells
18. A collection of blank books
19. Big turquoises: GSS his gift of a ring and the
    jewel sent by Judy Beltrametti
20. Portrait of P.W. by M. McClure (blue enamel on thick
    paper, 1959)

Start over in order to have a spare for each.

1-a. Collection of city maps, road maps &c

2-a. Silver dollar in plastic case, gift of Joe Brainard

3-a. The ingratitude!

4-a. I was happy to discover that I hadn't sold several books given to me by J-L. K.

5-a. Curious dream of thunder and lightning

6-a. I am drinking buttermilk while I write this

7-a. WHUMP!

8-a. Expensive sports glasses bought to watch kabuki from cheap seat; now used to observe sea lion, pelican sea gull conclaves on Duxbury Reef, also the moon

9-a. Septic tank crew and vacuum truck investigated the drains this morning . . . truck four times as big as those used in Kyoto

10-a. Yellow pansies in a whiskey glass, kitchen window bouquet; Joe LeMay sharpens his chain saw

11-a. New Korean brass incense burner. I couldn't get at any of those which I already own, an embarrassingly numerous collection

12-a. Japanese harness bell in the shape of a torus

13-a. Green soapstone image of Ganapati. Duerden says, "Give it to me when you die, will you?"

14-a. Pental sign pens in seven colors although black isn't a color

15-a. Forgotten kakemono, calligraphy of the late Kongo Abe

16-a. I can't remember anything about life in Japan. Zuishin-in, Daiho-onji, where at? How much did it cost to take a bath? 28 ¥

17-a. Forgot three-faced image in lacquer shrine as well as the small heavy Yamantaka image from China

18-a. If I were to write an autobiography what would I put in it?

19-a. I'm eating sunflower seeds

20-a. Collection of photos of P.W. from earliest childhood to the present

20-a-1. Red glass sanctuary light glows before Buddha

20-a-2. 1057 ¥ on deposit at the Sanjo Branch of the Sanwa Bank Kyoto, Nakagyoku, Sanjo-Kawaramachi-agaru. Its value increases daily increases daily

UN-GUM   UN-GUM   UN-GUM
UN-GUM   UN-GUM   UN-GUM
(African daisy mantra)
I call my powers to me
Crystals   colors   music
I begin to climb up
SING
up. UN-GUM! Crystals. UN-GUM! Power. UN-GUM! African Daisy.
UN-GUM! Colors. UN-GUM! The song of music.

(don't get hung up in any single chakra)

If the door knocks or the telephone rings
It's not my problem
UN-GUM!
What is the basis for your objection
Peanut brittle
UN-GUM!
Where would that put us.
UN-GUM!
Flute.   Oboe.   Viola d'amore.   Secret foods.   Oxygen.

H U M!

Outside as if suddenly happily naked
Top of my head painlessly removed
Effortless: beyond glad or tears in space beyond security outside
H U M!
The world really being I there
Lots of air the oceans and mountains
Bodega Bay sand cup hook
Waves can be heard and felt the whistle buoy also
Weimaraner puppy glad to see me again
Up beyond hope or wish or high
Z O P!

1–7:x:71

Occasional Dilemmas

What's perceived
DUCKRABBIT
nightjar (not a bird not a *vase de nuit* not the *Golden Bowl*)
BLUE
I applied the gentle but determined pressure of my right
forefinger to the mother-of-pearl button (the same as
total surveillance and repression).
If there was anyone within, he ignored the summons of the bell
which I could hear quite distinctly
NIGHTJAR
A bird   *vase de nuit*
a necessary vessel
I made certain of the address. It was difficult
to turn the thin pages of my address book, but I did not wish
to remove my gloves
RABBITDUCK
(reading from west to east)
The cocoa-fibre doormat seemed quite new. The porch lamp,
high and to the right of the bell-push, was made of frosted
orange glass cast into the shape of a torch flame. A closely
pleated green silk curtain stretched tightly across the thick
plate glass let into the center of the heavy front door.
In fine, the marvelously double vision: total security is
the same as total surveillance and repression.

Olson told us that history was ended.
> A.—"O.K. What is it you think you're doing?"
> B.—"I'm trying to wreck your mind, that's all."

30:xi:71–16:xii:71

Ode for You

What are you but a drifting crowd?
Miserable hermitage of dauby wattles
Flies ants bugs and busy rodents all over everything
Wrong climate for a primitive life out of doors
Wrong soil for a vegetable garden

Well, tell me about that.
No. No, it is too—
It is too boring to tell and I doubt that you have time
To listen.
What happened when you went to L.A.?

> At this point I shall draw a curtain of discretion
> across the scene and direct the attention of the
> reader to a large cardboard carton which stands
> on the floor
> beside the desk.

OBSCURANTISM

What about the hermitage. Where was it. When.

Grey clods of earth and bumptious weeds;
Dead batteries,

2.

This morning the ocean fits
Tight against the cliff

Mare's tails in the sky the weather will change
Prisms of Japanese quartz make rainbows on desk and bed
   "sealed in vain, sealed in vain"
    CHAIN SAW

the muddleheaded reader will inquire,
"What's the connection," poking about
with a long stick while crossing the moorlands—
when the point of the stick suddenly slides
into a hollow, start digging

(MALEBOLGE?)

Out come Little Cyril, Cousin Maude, the China pug dog,
Peacock feathers and gilded cattails, the player piano,
The cut-glass vinegar cruet, the Conductor (S.P. Railroad)
Darling Arabella,

3.

None of it is visionary or prophetickal
What's buried in earth is utterly used up
Ready to become flowers grassy weeping willow trees
Throw it all back
                    Other things are perfected underground
                    Onions and parsnips and diamonds;
                    Let us have those

We rise and fall through the earth
Geysers and artesian wells percolating
Through rocks from heaven's bright obstacles
            (hemisphere's balderdash)
Uncommonly streaked and splendid—
            so delicately—
650 pounds of marble

} N I K E {
white stone wings

17–20:xii:71

Alleyway

That darling baby!
All wrapped up asleep
In his fuzzy blue bunting
An extra blanket carefully pinned
Around him asleep on the ground
Between two boxes of rubbish
Beside the overflowing garbage cans
All alone. Throwed away.

3:i:72

In the Night

I keep hearing cars demons ghosts
Cars demons ghosts car demons
Quite naturally
The world is larger
More complicated than we can remember
And so we fall upward
Into a fake superiority

*

"I FUCKING RAN"

*

"elephant and sunset"

*

"huge hen"

*

Lots of speed makes the surfboard slicker
Falling upward

*

THE WARS OF ONAN

*

We die reading about worrying about
Our lives

ONIN-NO-RAN (1467–1475)
Lots of speed. I fucking ran.

Civil wars more interesting than any other kind
AMERICA

8–12:i:72

"Stolen and Abandoned"

It's all back up in there
Floor's awash
"Anchor the way"
Angkor's this way back up over there:
Flesh awash unlimited satin
Waters of the sea
        (OUT OF SIGHT)
Abandonment by stealth. Adornments of good health.
Worthless self. Rub my feet.
       (patte de mouche)
Rub my back. No wonder you're not sleepy
The moon is full and you're all wired up
(On one cup of tea?) Completely wired.

Give up. Give up everything.
    STUDENT: "What keeps us from giving up everything?"
    TEACHER: "Fiction."
Wild applause
(mild applesauce, upside down)
        id est,
          notions of loss and disaster all attract
          demons ghosts and depressions: bum vibes
          create atmosphere for mistaken happening
          "accident." Fear of planning because there
          may be disappointment ("no plan" equals
          "freedom"?). There turns out to be a secret
          plan, a wordless design framed by "character."
          "Then" becomes "now" rather than present
          intention governing the future. (?) Pattern
          without words equals "mandala" which is one
          single troublesome image? (But recall five
          several personal body images during Kyoto
          psilocybin trip. Have I been seeing some-
          thing backwards or upside down?)

O sharp cumbersome Death!
Most of us tire of thinking and feeling
We fall asleep. Reb is asleep
Head in a tiger's mouth.

20:vii–13:x:72

Tassajara

What I hear is not only water but stones
No, no, it is only compressed air flapping my eardrums
My brains gushing brown between green rocks all
That I hear is me and silence
The air transparent golden light (by Vermeer of Delft)
Sun shines on the mountain peak which pokes
The sun also ablaze &c.
Willard Gibbs, Hans Bethe, what's the answer
A lost mass (Paris gone)
Shine red in young swallow's mouth
Takagamine Road

The water suffers
Broken on rocks worn down by water
Wreck of THE DIVINE MIND on the reef called Norman's Woe
"Suddenly, ignorance," the *Shastra* says.
Moon arises in my big round head
Shines out of my small blue eyes
Tony Patchell hollers "Get it! Get it!"
All my treasure buried under Goodwin Sands

20:vii–25:xi:72

The Universal &
Susquehanna Mercy Co. Dayton, O.

Everybody downtown
Miserable today
Bought the wrong size
Overdrawn at the bank

The spots were there before the leopard
Now explain the panther
Sun reflected in black
Tar pools

"American society"—great dead animal carcase
We try to bury it, forget it
We carve steaks off it and get indigestion
Some of us walk away

Death's ivory
Buck tooth skull
Stone says "I will never live"
Snake: "I'll never die"

All the wrong people rush up to me
Screeching, "You're a poet you're a
Poet you're a Great POET!"
Time to move on. Complete disconnection
Misunderstanding brought on by overpayment

In X-ville California
People swept under the rug
Living sow bug lives
The Dormition of the Virgin
(What a word, also an oil painting or so)
Alice in Wonderland
Bichloride of mercury

Try to reorder your scrambled head & broken eyes
Apply vanilla milkshake anti-paranoia compound
No possibility of escape
Two sets of electrically charged barbwire
The Trojan War continues, the Iliad is unfinished
No sales tax on flame throwers
What's possible? Bandages? Paint?

26:v:72–25:iv:73

Message

                    yesterday,
from sudden red lily
          Amaryllis
              (Naked Lady)
THE YEAR IS DYING
        leafless and red
              bright as rhubarb
Uninvited lily
        (what bulb so dim
              what Dora so dumb
Not to see sun's heat
        snow's white)
        howling flower in my skull

14–16:vii:73

High-tension on Low-pressure Non-accomplishment Blues

Dog's laughing mouth and happy eye
No-color fur brown eyes white teeth red tongue
Dripping. Its lips are black
Precisely notched
OPTICAL INSTRUMENT HANDLE WITH CARE
(Optical instrument no longer there)
Nothing to be done with that picture, either:
Precise image of wood grain in bare *engawa* floor
I could feel and smell it and behind me the garden
The tree peonies a single rock for a step and
Dirt with moss and pebbles
Hot sun illuminates plaster wall
(precisely blocked)
Every morning I am fat
Every morning I am old
Every morning bought and sold

what may have been thought of once
as a snappy summer hat supposedly hand woven
dirty mole-colored plastic fiber on top of hair
partly dyed dark red above skin
almost the right complexion for that kind of hair
perfectly white very short bristles
mark out a new square moustache
irresistible charm
has got to be good for something

16:viii–26:ix:73

Mask

A carved living wood face
You can see exactly where it lies in the living tree
Which now goes about as the tree's ghost also person
Gold flat circular eyes
You see the tree
There sun wind
Throwing branches and the mask
Growing under the bark
Twisting and swaying
Always alive

6:xii:73

Detachment, Wisdom and Compassion

"... had it to do
all over again ..."

      (an oval window
      no longer there)

"O if only I had it to do ..."

"They took and messed with it
Until I had it all to do over
Again; they'd made such a hash of it."

      and cleverly steps to the left
      as the 500 pound falling sandbag
      makes a thump dent in the solid oak floor
      (unthinking) right beside him
         ("no longer there")

8:xii:73

Money Is the Roost of All Eagles

Instant milk and then I saw
Insistent milk
But love is not love
That altercation finds

* * * * * *

Instantaneously silk?

* * * * * *

Alteration finds instantly
    M I L K
    ?

* * * * * *

Love is not milk (alternation)
    F I E N D S!

* * * * * *

    innocent eagle

12:iii:74

"The Conditions That Prevail"

TRANSVESTITE
    1) (The heavy gold chain loops) across
the sung-fitting waistcoat (snug)

Today I am the SOKU, butler/head waiter three times today
Today Elemental Powers gnomes and gremlins catch
Heels and jog elbows. Conspicuous minor hysteria.

TRAMPOLINE
        1) bright yellow crystals of barium sulfate
        2) vaseline and boric acid

TRANSVESTITE
        2) a phase of silicon perchloride occurring
        as lilac-coloured rhomboidal crystals on a
        matrix of pure natural tin

Today I act as KOKYO (precentor)
Have you seen the platter of little feet?

Today I am supposed to be the DOAN (gong klonger)
But I lost my temper during the morning service
Lost all recollection of the schedule and my various duties
Missed breakfast, God knows who played the Buddha drum
While I was finding out who was Wanshi Sogaku
In the wrong kind of Chinese transliteration

25:ii–17:iii:74

255

The Talking Picture

Watching the tail end of a film running through the projector
Gate—blackness, random design, blackness, a few numbers,
Blackness a pattern blip blackness
                    LIGHT
Square and clicking as loose film end
Whips against projector housing
Click frequency dropping as take-up reel slows to a stop.
The projector motor keeps on humming I watch
A square of light until power switch
Clicks total blackness

13:iv:74

Dream Poems

1.

Let me see:
The original sinful. By virtue of
The power invested in me

> (Glenway Westcoat)

     I declare
Give me turtle death
Not in the usual way; underneath

> (Lucille)

   R A M P A G E
Let me know when the crew table is ready
(How sad the whole day's gone)
     D O T
         (do I)
  (do it?)
     bring me there immediately
Immoderately
    SLURM   SLURM   SLURM
Let's take the Graham-Page

2.

Nobody's hand appears in the air
Shroud clouds at wrist amid fog outside window
Three storeys above the street
To tap my bedroom window
I turn to face my father who sits in small upholstered chair
Looking directly towards the window
"Do you see it?
Have you ever seen anything like that?" (I feel
Outraged) "A disembodied hand tapping the window?"
But he can't hear me, being dead in the graveyard
Up in Mosier makes four too many levels of reality
That I can't handle. O I dreamed yes
Yes I dreamed
That.

30–31:v:74

Murals Not Yet Dreamed

The First Panel is occupied with Storm and Night Battle:
Handsome Allegorical Embellishments fruits and flowers
Antique masks and fantastic animals or birds amid trailing
    vines and scallop shells, leaves, Wild Men, Trophies,
    Instruments of Music profusely beribboned and garlanded
The whole supported on sculptured brackets or consoles
Decorated with partially draped Atlantids wreathed with
    oaken crowns

The Second Panel shews the arrival of the King
And the fit is on him
He shouts for the Countess of Suffolk who lies ill in her room
Lord Townshend, Sir Robert Walpole and the Duke of
    Newcastle
Approach from the right, bearing a petition
Sir Robert stares into the clear blue eyes of Queen Caroline
Dressed in seventy or eighty yards of handmade Flemish lace and
Silk brocade, a young fortune in pearls and diamonds and a couple
Of egret feathers. Lord Hervey as Vice Chamberlain preens
And simpers at her side all blue velvet and lavender silk

The Third Panel crashes down in splinters and torn canvas
I open fire with my Sten gun, screeching defiance
As they mow me down.

11–12:vi:74

258

The Vision of Delight

The man driving the expensive car
May have been no relation to the woman sitting beside him
Neither of them might be related to the small girl
Who sat in the center of the back seat, leaning immobile
Against the back rest.
Her dress was white her hair all neatly arranged
Grotesque white fangs protruded from her mouth
Without distorting it.
She looked serenely straight ahead.
She was the queen attended by court lady and chauffeur
Not going to the Safeway store, clearly not needing
The automobile, who can appear anywhere any time
Such is her tremendous power

21:vii:74

Luxury in August

Not you but your beauty:
What a waste of time.
Tooth of August white sun flare
    Teedle-dee-dum dum deedle
Your moon head shining
Catamount cold eye glow
                dum dee dum
The *Surangama Sutra* says,
    "Creatures through whom the future can be foretold
    after repaying their former debts
    are reborn as literary men"
              boppity mop.

17:viii:74

How to Be Successful & Happy
Without Anybody Else Finding
Out About It

I was falling asleep in my chair
Now I lie on the floor, ruminating ideas of life's brevity
The feeble intensity of enormous ambition
Hasleton Brasler said he'd be over
He had to pick up his car and take a haircut
You understand what I'm talking about . . .
            "including the power tools"
There's no excuse for an imitation of Billie Holiday.

Think of grass, a half acre of weeds, lawn, eucalyptus trees
Pink lilies on leafless thick red stems, all in a row
Appearing "spontaneously" (not from a regular bed or trench
Of specially cultivated earth. You remember what I'm talking
About, you've been there, but maybe not in lily season)

A freezing cold morning, throat and sinuses "burning"
Hasleton Brasler was uncertain: Thursday or Saturday.
He didn't want tea or whiskey. He had forgotten why he
   wanted to see me.

My sleep wrecked with difficult dreams,
Managing crowds of friends, trying to organize them
Interrupted (wakened) by scene with (who?) again
Persuade, explain, hopeless
The lilies shove right up out of the grass
Where one expects flat ground, these big
Vegetable telephone rockets, their irregular line
Fat rutabaga bulbs clearing the surface of the ground
Swelling and subdividing

Probably listening to Hasleton Brasler last night
Trying to come up with helpful suggestions for "coping" with

his difficulties.
With so little rain the lilies will be late this year.
Why don't I go home to Oregon?
Seventy or eighty feet of "naked ladies" all in a row: Amaryllis

> "... brought the apples you wanted ...
>> ... more tomorrow," Theocritus says.

6:ix:74

Compulsive Obligatory
Paranoia Flashes

While ever at my back I hear Time's winged chariot,
More or less skillfully guided by Henry and Claire Booth Luce
He (Agni, the Hindu god of fire) said,
"Why have ye (Devas) brought me to birth?"
They answered, "To keep watch."

Tomatoes must be gently wrapped in suitable coverings
And shut up in a dark place like mad men
Where they ripen

The world is a willful Idea? I'm after something;
Bright changing shadow
(Everything to eat except desire)

"The last time I saw him his face and head
Were completely depilated and all his features gross
And swollen like Gene Sibelius."
"*Jean,*" somebody said. "Or *Jan?*"
"What are you, some kind of intellectual?"

September–December 1974

For Clark Coolidge

tick

notch

fanrandole

A Venetian lantern rhyme

Perfume wild thyme gland of youth

Clara Wilkes Booth, Founderess

Red Cross and Salvation Army

Clara Barton Batten Durstine & Osborn

incunabula tightrope novel of blank mind

born clear and smooth   not a wedge in sight

whelms. qualms. nick.

(*scotch*)

sham

5:vi:75

The Radio Again

It wasn't in the cards
That today should go the way I want
Not in the cards.
I can't complain about the way it went.

   "It says right on the box"
           as her voice tells us her name is Ethel

Lady, it is what the lawyers call a self-serving document

   "Oh yes, I always buy this kind."

Voice, tell us
The name of the earth.

November 1975–January 1976

Somebody Else's Problem Bothers Me

Warm sun and chilly air, water is low and the creek is clear
Will I accidentally drop a jade ring in the creek
All the new stones glaring light and airplanes
Shall I drop my gold crown in the pool?
Have I derailed my train of thought?
A rock with an elephant's forehead!
Silver turquoise ring dropped into monk's kimono sleeve
What can we answer?

Yellow tin chimneys.

White-crowned sparrows.

Everything a-tilt.

26:iii:76

Bead

Aimless
Wet finger no foresight
Small craft warning from Telephone Company
Earth
Bear
> Birth
> O
> Breath
> and
> Bread
(Careless wet finger again)

28:iii:76

Defective Circles

Electric clock died in the night
Big low-pressure system high winds and rain barge through
Present world, wake up in the dark 12:05
". . . made by magic no handmakers know . . ."
Shall I remember that when I get back from the bathroom?
Lines of groovy poem around me
Did I know who I was where then?
12:05 daylight, don't care much about who I am
What I'm supposed to be doing
Still humming and warm to the touch
Neither of us making any sense.

12:iii:77

Obsolete Models

Now the hours of my life grow small
Shoddy months and threadbare years
A favorite pet universe that ought to be "put to sleep"
By the vet; gracefully relinquished.

I say, "Something eludes me
Something is right over there—someplace."

A drop of mercury slides very smoothly away
A description slightly out of focus

At least there are nasturtiums again
Disc leaves dusty green
More entertaining than many another
Verdigris

What do I want
What am I really after
Sometimes a tree answers.

San Francisco, 18–19:iv:77

Many Pages Must Be Thrown Away

To talk about the green roof
Next to the silvery blue house—pointless
Because the way the light hits them
There are more colors anyhow—
Porpoise flank, eye of albacore

Air all new and clean
Sharp edges of Berkeley reappear
Among bridge cable web and thrum
Sundown crosslight bird clank
City Hall dome throbs and bulges
Opera House whale eyes look west
Suave white geometry lid of cathedral
Translucent, incandescent

I ascend to the roof to look again
Light as it is at Tangiers, they say,
Straight across walls doors hills

Against which waves flash explode eastward
Ocean rushing toward Donner Pass

14–23:iv:77

The Congress of Vienna

What's happening continues
"All still going on out there"
Last night eclipsed the moon
In order to say "Earth is a celestial disc
Over—not under—the moon"

Let's reconvene the Congress of Vienna
Nasturtiums at Schoenbrunn
Posies for Prince Metternich
Nosegays for Prince Talleyrand

On the floor a platter of chicken,
Thin elegant gravy, all of us eating
Most of us resigned to having a third helping
Long-haired grey cat walks into the dish, lies down
Rolls about in the sauce
Universal horror and chagrin!
We try to clean it with a big bath towel
If it licks up too much gravy the cat will have the gout
Annoyance, mirth, and worry
As long as I do not look out the window,
Great things, weird sounds,
High deeds in Lily Alley:
"You there track book!
Brat work! Dropsy!
Dim attending brunt or charred bird."
"What did you have for dinner?"
"Chard quiche."
"Hey there! 1878!"
"Eighteen seventy ate three, hey? There."
Quick change cymbal
". . . the difference to me!"

What though my eyes are blind with age and simple mindedness?
Death's crumby fingers insinuating fate

Tumescent sentences to say, to want to say,
"Flower: The world here becomes pond lilies
Tall yellow iris and trade for a world of rhododendrons
Total experience of wealth beyond rich and poor
Monterey cypress and black pine cliffs
Birdshadows trill and marble hallelujah
Out beyond the throne of time.

San Francisco, 4:iv–11:v:77

To the Memory Of

Mr J who had been poor for years
Inherited all the money in the world
Bought a gun to blow a hole in his head
To let in air and light he said
To let me out

Today, I have my head to shave
There are lights and shadows in it
All too soon empty open ashes
Join mirthfully to earth

19:v:77

"Past Ruin'd Ilion"

Past ancient dusty Antigua bright blue water above Port Royal
Beyond Terre Haute the legendary city
Abandoned to the winds of moon by Tom Field and Cubby Selby
Olson said that Cubby Selby walked up the road all alone
Wearing a baseball glove, tossing a ball in the air
As he approached the campus of Black Mountain College
Left his luggage at the station to await developments
If it wasn't Cubby Selby it was that guy
Who later wrote his recollections of Franz Kline
So much for reminiscences of the great
   "Tossing a ball in the air and catching it. Beautiful."

It probably was Fielding Dawson
Anyway, somebody burned down Pass Christian, Mississippi
Probably not Hubert Selby, Jr
Past the barriers of time and the ruining of Denver
The demolition of Portland (Oregon)
The voice of Nellie Melba echoing in the Parthenon
Sara Bernhardt at the Erechtheum Judy Garland
At the Orpheum
Viciously entangled; everything deliberately scrambled
There is complete exact beauty and satisfaction
Even the empty shells are beautiful to contemplate,

          (DESUNT CETERA)

Port Townsend, 11–12 July 1977

Tears and Recriminations

How charming the sticky sweat
The overheated stove the deranged sensibilities
The lady student suspended from College as
"Morally insensate"
As two lovely oranges in a little basket lined with a folded
Red linen napkin

". . . but only if it gratifies your inmost wish," I said
And the saltine being smeared with peanut butter
Broke in two

Tassajara, 5:ii:78

Discriminations

Earliest morning hot moonlight
A catastrophe, the garden too theatrical
Feels wild, unearthly
H. P. Lovecraft could use his favorite adjective:
"Eldritch"

The "shooting-star" flowers that Mama used to call "bird-bills"
Bloom around the Hogback graveyard
Suzuki Roshi's great seamless monument
Wild cyclamen, actually, as in the *Palatine Anthology*
I go home to mend my *rakusu* with golden thread.

Tassajara, 24:ii:78

Homage to St. Patrick, García Lorca, & the Itinerant Grocer

FOR M-D. SCHNEIDER

A big part of this page (a big part of my head)
Is missing. That cabin where I expected to sit in the
Woods and write a novel got sold
     out from under my imagination

I had it all figured out
     in the green filter of a vine-maple shade
The itinerant grocer would arrive every week
There was no doubt in my mind that I'd have money
To trade for cabbages and bread

Where did that vision take place—maybe Arizona
     Or New Mexico, where trees are much appreciated—

I looked forward to having many of my own
Possessed them in a nonexistent future green world of lovely prose
Lost them in actual present poems in Berkeley
All changed, all strange, all new; none green.

Tassajara, 17:iii:78

What About It?

When I began to grow old I searched out the Land
Of the Gods in the West, where our people have always said it is.
Once I floated there on the water. Once I flew there.
I heard their music and saw the magic dancing.
They appeared in many shapes; once as *kachina,*
Once I could only see shining feet and radiant clothes
Their houses blend into water, trees and stone.
A curtain moved. Water fell in certain order.
Sometimes there was a great mirror of polished bronze.
Other messages were smell of *hinoki, sugi,* gingko
Newly watered stones.
The land itself delivers a certain intelligence.

How embarrassing to note that four days are gone.
All I can say right now is I can see clouds in the sky
If I stand still and look out the window.
Diane Di Prima came and told me, "If we leave
Two hours of the day open for them
The poems will come in or out or however;
Anyway, to devote time in return for a place
That makes us accessible to them."

San Francisco, 17–28:iv:78

Treading More Water

It is very hard to understand that
We are where we are at; I am here intentionally
Can you want to do anything
What were you doing. Standing around talking
Greater downtown Chehalis
Night or late-blooming seriously
Let us fall back and regroup (Laocoön)

The mad King of Ireland
Suibhne could fly
That is flying was a symptom of his madness
He lived in a tree; he ate nothing at all.
Crowned.

Start again. Direct the imagination
A knotted mass of grey yarn and very delicate blood vessels
Forward (there's no other direction)
Enclosed please find the pig
"fantastically dressed up with flowers"
"mad, crowned with weeds and flowers"
"mad, bedecked with weeds"
"mad, (fantastically dressed with weeds)"

Seven minutes from now. You hear the words.
"Caught between Sybil and Charisma"
I am grown invisible and very wise

San Francisco, 11:vii:78

279

Treading Water

insist there be a voice, then listen

*

X: "You can do everything."
Y: "I'm so glad. One day,
   I shall buy a full gallon of Best Foods Mayonnaise."

*

Budweiser: used egg
New bicycle. Proudly.
   Who.

*

X: Wouldn't it be strange
   Never to go back to that building
   Revisit (for example) New Mexico
   Or Kyoto every year, commencing now.
Y: Whatever for? & why "strange"?
   There's no reason to go back—you didn't
   Leave your hat, or lose your watch?
X: Monstrous. Gross. Un-natural.
   Love comes back to dote and sigh,
   "If only . . ."

*

The orphan scottie didn't quite follow me out the door—whether he's
   getting used to the idea that he shouldn't run out into the street . . .
   was he discouraged by the sight of that steep brick stairway or was
   he resigned to the idea that I (like his recent master) was abandoning
   him—who knows? I worry about that dog, unable to care sincerely

about little else beyond the pleasure of writing it here.
The dog is helpless, fat, and lost; seemingly aware that he's temporarily
safe and generally admired, but not particularly loved? no specific (as
once two) person(s) he must love in return;

*

X: Where has caring gone.
Y: Back to Montana, in a Volkswagen bug.

*

I love you very much
But sometimes I love you even more from a distance
Never to the vanishing point

*

It's true, as Duncan used to say,
We need permission for what we do
Next we must grab permission by the horns & hang on
It isn't just a grant, a gift, a boon, grab it and run
Before they change their minds
                    PARCAE
                    MOIRA
Hang on while he goes through all
His demonic changes,
Old what's his name, out of the sea
Will be obliged to say what's true
If you can keep hold and listen.
You see only flashing in the air from the jewels
That I'm wearing a bear triangle upside down
Gold and silver sleep; diamonds wake.
I see you in spite of my wrinkled eyes

*

Now the little dog is attached by his leash to the leg of a yellow
upholstered wing-chair in the Flop Room. He lies on the floor, most of
the time, dejected—and sensible of a general (if gentle) rejection.
Some dog enthusiasts cart him out for a walk but they bring him back too
soon and set him in the corner again like a fern. There he must await
developments. He has clean water in a yellow plastic dish. The dish is
probably clean enough for a dog but it looks dingy and sad. The dog's
various wounds, received in a recent fight, have been treated several
times by a vet and are healing.

There is food and care and endlessly interrupted and scattered attention.
The little dog seems indifferent—doped and sad. Lucy says she's doing
her best to find a home for him. Why does his appearance trouble me.
He's only a dog, and everything that can be done for him is being done.

10:vi–8:viii:78

What? Writing in the Dining Room?

One long table supported by three sets of winged lions;
Each lion has a single, enormous clawed foot
Their faces resemble those of American highschool students
Expressing rage, horror, disbelief
Here might be kings and commissars affixing signatures and seals
To important documents of state.

I imagine a dream recollection of my father
Telling his mother-in-law a plan of collecting 50¢ per night
From every guest in his house.
Hot northwind flaps my clothes.

Is there a way whereby I can stop stoning myself
Get on with my work? I want to write this
I refuse to do anything else as long as I want to
Write this it is important and horrible and meaningless. . . .

There.
"DON'T MOVE"
i.e. by not moving I lend some shade
make a lap for the baby or for the cat
My shoes are set in a row, not going anywhere
As if I'd gone without them
Carted directly to hospital or morgue
To little magic nonexistent worlds
Pagan Rome
Nothing reappeared; two is lost
"The time has come and went," she said
Unable to keep our engagement for lunch

The little dog has gone to live in Visalia.
Everybody misses him, of course.

15–24:ix:78

What's New?

We keep forgetting the world is alive
Being the same as we
The coathanger and kimono leap off the rail
Hurl themselves to the floor
Instead of the usual instant anger
I pause to admire this prodigy of nature
The kimono flowing in strange billows and festoons
Falling timelessly (if I say so) to the closet floor.

A couple weeks later I'm flailing about
The rug rippled and ruched, table cockeyed
Something tips over, I (furious) grab, rush,
Breathless dark living room
Why can't you, what's to stop your doing
Whatever you want to do—collect SOMETHING
Fill in the blanks later, unexpected brilliant excursions
And back again to the central trunk or channel

Watching the "waterfall" (more accurately, "water curtain")
In Beale St. PGE has done something to my head
I see myself, all persons, animals, trees &c
FALLING through space, dividing and disintegrating
Halfway down, some are shattered on the first step of the "fall"
Fragments thrown into the narrow pool next below "inevitably"
And then pumped, I suppose, to some tank or pool (roof garden?)
Above.

I like to think there's a garden and pond,
Plain green shrubs, maybe azaleas or camellias in tubs
Doors from the company restaurant open onto it
The pond a formal baroque design as at Inoda Coffee Shop in Kyoto
White smooth concrete framing it, mechanical but pleasing
("Grooming displacement behavior"?)

After murdering Kesa Gozen—by his own mistake
But her design—Endo Morito stood under the waterfall
Three weeks in a row, invoking Fudo Myo-o
And came out as Mongaku Shonin the famous monk
Who went really crazy with political intrigue
Lost everything at last and died in exile,
Sado Island, 1193.

4,27:xii:78

Violins in Chaos?

Yes, now I go ahead,
Words appear and all a living world beside:
Not exactly a peak-out but a distinct blip
On an otherwise flat curve
Knobby leaf mud curtain grows on steep rock
Then lichens, moss, ferns, in Darwinian succession
A tough wide-leaved succulent lays down on top
To hide the details

OLDE SONG: "I went &
{ closed the window
pulled the curtain
put out the light

So he shouldn't see my Fancy"

I didn't remember to say, that
The most brilliant white light sounds
Like the shattering of a huge pane of glass
Water makes neat crystal helmet over the rock

Tassajara, 20–22:i:79

286

The Bay Trees Were About to Bloom

For each of us there is a place
Wherein we will tolerate no disorder.
We habitually clean and reorder it,
But we allow many other surfaces and regions
To grow dusty, rank and wild.

So I walk as far as a clump of bay trees
Beside the creek's milky sunshine
To hunt for words under the stones
Blessing the demons also that they may be freed
From Hell and demonic being
As I might be a cop, "Awright, move it along, folks,
It's all over, now, nothing more to see, just keep
Moving right along"

I can move along also
"Bring your little self and come on"
What I wanted to see was a section of creek
Where the west bank is a smooth basalt cliff
Huge tilted slab sticking out of the mountain
Rocks on the opposite side channel all the water
Which moves fast, not more than a foot deep,
Without sloshing or foaming.

Tassajara, 11:ii:79

Dying Tooth Song

Now flesh and bones burn inside my mouth
Ganges gushes from under my tongue
To fall in Siva's hair
Tooth temple of Kali
Skull dance place of Siva

Becoming Yama god of death
I become Yamantaka slayer of death
Endless wheel of waterbuckets turns
Through Babylon zodiac

I stays here turning through life and death
Offering up all this flesh and bones
Round and round

Grass greener than yellower
More birds than bluejays
Railway roar of creek
Not going to Chicago

North mountain peak
A pile of patriarchs' bones
Nyogen, Shunryu, host and guest all one heap

Tassajara, 28:ii:79

Rich Interior, After Thomas Mann

Why, as I was walking up the hill,
All in spring light and air
Keep seeing a glass of water standing
On a polished wooden tabletop in a big house at twilight?
As the air warms, flies and bugs hatch out
Come to sit on top of this page, O.K.?

2.

Yesterday's glass of water:
Standing on bare wood—surely
This was carelessly done!
There'll be a ring.
Of course, rubbing it with lemon oil will remove the mark?
This house is one cared for by "a lady who comes in" daily.
Presently it is her hand which conveys the glass
Through the next couple of handsomely furnished rooms
To the kitchen; the same hand will bring the lemon oil.
An imperfect white ring about 3/8ths of an inch wide
And almost the exact diameter of the glass
Shows where it stood. A stain.

Tassajara, 3–4:iii:79

Chanson d'Outre Tombe

They said we was nowhere
Actually we are beautifully embalmed
    in Pennsylvania
They said we wanted too much.
Gave too little, a swift hand-job
      no vaseline.
We were geniuses with all kinds
    embarrassing limitations
O if only we would realize our potential
O if only that awful self-indulgence
& that shoddy politics of irresponsibility
O if only we would grow up, shut up, die
& so we did & do & chant beyond
     the cut-rate grave digged by
       indignant reviewers
O if we would only lay down & stay
    THERE—In California, Pennsylvania
Where we keep leaking our nasty radioactive
  waste like old plutonium factory
Wrecking your white expensive world

Tassajara, 27:iii:1979

Hot Springs Infernal in the Human Beast

Examine a big stone across the creek outside the kitchen window
Instead of walking out to coffee? Saved by the real world again!
Walk.
Get away from here? Go read thermometer in the garden;
Fingernails unaccountably dirty.

      hummingbird

I gross and unwiedly, torpid and silent
I must begin to flap new plumes, great wings
And sing a one-eyed song of Halicarnassus in the spring
Old and immense and hastening to die
Clutch wildly at any spark of life

      hummingbird

Yellow anemone
Purple morning Glory
Four nasturtiums (O R A N G E)

Tassajara, 5:x:79

Homage to Hart Crane

As golden yellow as possible
The rocks blue-green as T'ang Dynasty
Clothing colors mudded out—red, yellow, blue, green, black
Animals, imaginary lions, elephants and tigers
Realistic birds. I need a big collection of Crayolas.

Image flowers in mirror landscape sexier
Under glass, poem or picture
Reflection statuary reflecting lights and images
Are there many places.
Only by looking at small details of moss or flower centers
Through a magnifying glass

"uncathected Oedipal backlash; schizoid mirror worlds of brilliant silence"

Now I find I've skipped all carelessly onto this page
Leaving the opening preceding this one blank
Fetch the colors! Summon the genius!

Restriction of the view by round window frame
Lends something of the thick
Unobtainable silence of mirrors
When looking at a distant landscape from a great height
Something of the same feeling occurs
The part of the world "over there," mountains &c
Is absolutely silent
While the place where one stands is nearly still.
Hell yes.
A distinct blue line. The thread of the discourse
Tightens up too much; puckers the fabric.

Tassajara, 23–26:x:79

292

What Are You Studying, These Days?

The electronic watch runs backwards to five A.M.
At night I read with broken eyes
How to control the Universe: compel with mantra, mandala, vision—
Summon, seal, dissolve, bind, subjugate & destroy &c
Powers to do what is already being done anyway
"Power to do good," or "Sufficient unto the day is the evil thereof"
"Sweet Analytics, 'tis thou hast ravish'd me"

The Merry-go-round, the Ferris Wheel
The shoot-the-chutes

Your trouble is you're not very real, are you.
Hallucinatory fountain pens, eh?
Skin chips and flaky on the outside
Internal organs all blackened and shriveled
What do you expect with too much in mind
Too busy to see or hear a single particular?
I have put on a gown of power I didn't know I had—
Or wanted.

Tassajara, 20:xi:79

Dharmakaya

The real thing is always an imitation
Consider new plum blossoms behind the zendō

20:i:81

Some of These Days

I

AND THIS THAT IS WEDNESDAY

Rain greases all false lips. Earth quacks
       in Hollister & Watsonville
        {"Ducky falls, lips"}
          30 miles south of San Jose'
        {"Poor Joseph!"}

   Where am I at. "Depend on the kindness
          of strangers"

          *
        * *

Dumb fatality!

          *
        * *

How much trouble would it take in order
to gain civil or military control of San Francisco?

          *
        * *

Downtown rain dim lonesome bar no music yet
(what it means is my life as a young soldier)
  Steak dinner, drunk hotel room,
         free doughnut & coffee breakfast
              South Dakota
              too far from the ocean

          *
        * *

28:i:81

I I

MORE WEDNESDAY?

Thursday's insistences press
               Wednesday inside a sausage casing

Be very careful with any given moment, e.g.
"What did I tell you. Tie the string
           around your overcoat button . . ."

Expensive Balloon already sailing above the department store

S C R E E C H !

*
  * *

Now a giant kettle of irresistable soup
One dish of good soup deserves another
              Red wine.

*
  * *

28:i:81

I I I

THURSDAY

What machine am I talking to
    {ADDRESSOGRAPH}

Thursday major
    Thursday of the Chaldees

Utterly hopeless little sounds of chaos & dismay
{". . . The number you have reached is out of
service at this time . . . this is a recording."}
                    honey-crazed melopath

                         *
                    *   *

The arms of Morpheus: Proper closed eyes
sable or.

                         *
                    *   *

who's been swimming
    in the olive oil?   did that spoil anything?

        {soothe}   {grimace}

                         *
                    *   *

                        LOSS

                    *   *
                         *

        "Swivel," I thought, forgetting the tears
    the painful contretemps, the savage recriminations,

                                                    29:i:81

                        I V

                    THURSDAY, TOO

    There are more days than usual in January
    There are fewer days in old Thibet

waltz can you fry a clam, bake an egg, tap a
song lamb, grope a leg/can you bounce a duck
Maurice slice a corn, roll a drunk, die forlorn?
Ravel

   More days than enough in Cincinnatti
   What do you do with all your time
   What's your story
   February is too short to explain
   Let us cart you off to Egypt
      all time lives there

   groom your brain, sort your wits,
   prop your smile, miss your plane, smooth your head
   shave your pits, work with guile, don't complain

       *

   swift spoilage due to refrigeration failure

       *

      LOSS

       *

   "Now my days are swifter than a post"

       *

     a relapse.

29:i:81

V

THURSDAY, THREE

We dream of our ancestors, then it rains
Your ancestors are books or museum exhibits
        protected by mechanical weather
I can't imagine dreaming of the 11th volume
        of Plutarch's Moralia—

A Greek vase, a Sumerian seal,
        a carved jade might appear
Hand-made objects with something alive
        about them
    But no rain

Only seagull grandpa can find it
    I see him.

        *
      * *

        And we are sorry for you.
        INTERNATIONAL SOCIETY OF
        SHAMANS, WARLOCKS & INDE-
        PENDENT TRIBESMEN OF THE
        PAGAN OR HEATHEN KIND, INC.

        * *
        *

29:i:81

Epigrams & Imitations

I
ACTIONS OF BUDDHA

Clip cuticle; drink orange juice
"be confirmed by 10,000 things"
(the next line after that is delinquent)
        turtles

I I
UPON THE POET'S PHOTOGRAPH

This printed face doesn't see
A curious looking in;
Big map of nothing.

I I I
FROM THE JAPANESE OF KAKINOMOTO HITOMARO

What though my shorts are threadbare
I deserve all your love

I V
FALSE *SENRYŪ*

A cough
waits for the bus.

V
PERPETUUM MOBILE

Everybody has a car
But something's wrong with it
We are going very fast—
Have you noticed
The driver is a headless corpse

V I
THE CONCEALED PHOENIX
TREASURE JEWEL TERRACE,
AFTER LI HO

Mountains dream tigers and monkeys
The sea imagines dragons
Monstrous birds trouble the air.
The moon bothers all & sundry,
with or without reflection.

1981

For Allen, on His 60th Birthday

Having been mellow & wonderful so many years
What's left but doting & rage?
Yet the balance of birthing & dying
Keeps a level sight: Emptiness, not
Vacancy, has room for all departure &
Arrival; I don't even know what
Day it is.

28:viii:85

BIBLIOGRAPHY

*

Three Satires. Portland, Ore.: Privately published, 1951.
 Wrappers. 13 copies.
Song. Portland, Ore.: Privately published, 1951.
Self-Portrait from Another Direction. San Francisco: Auerhahn Press, 1959.
The End, of a Month of Sundays. San Francisco: Auerhahn Press, 1959.
 Wrappers.
NOTE: 1. Cover title of only "Auerhahn Press" for this folded broadside, which is also
  encountered with wrappers.
  2. John Wieners, Philip Lamantia and Michael McClure.
  3. Commonly referred to by Wieners's title, "Bag Dad by the Bay."
Memoirs of an Interglacial Age. San Francisco: Auerhahn Press, 1960. 51 pp.
 Two issues, no priority:
  1. Hardcover, no priority:
   a. 60 copies.
   b. 25 copies, with an original drawing and holograph poem by the author.
   c. 15 copies, signed by the author.
From Memoirs of an Interglacial Age. Cambridge, Mass. Paterson, ca. 1960.
 Mimeographed sheet.
Like I Say. New York: Totem Press/Corinth Books, 1960. 47 pp.
 Gray wrappers.
 Publishers' names on copyright page.

Hymnus Ad Patrem Sinensis. San Francisco: San Francisco Arts Festival Commission, 1963.
>Broadside.
>300 copies, most of which were signed by the author.
NOTE: Laid in portfolio entitled "San Francisco Arts Festival: A Poetry Folio: 1963."
Three Mornings. San Francisco: Four Seasons Foundation, 1964.
>Broadside.
Monday, in the Evening, 21:vii:61. Milan: Privately published, 1964.
>Wrappers, no priority:
>1. 291 copies, numbered.
>2. 18 copies, hors commerce.
Goddess. San Francisco: Don Carpenter, 1964.
>Broadside, no priority:
>1. 100 copies.
>2. 25 copies without colophon, for the use of the author.
Dear Mr. President. San Francisco: Impressions Production, 1965.
>Broadside.
>1. 500 copies.
Every Day. Eugene, Ore.: Coyote's Journal, 1965.
>Wrappers.
>Coyote Book #1.
>1. 500 copies.
>Second Printing: Ann Arbor, 1965. 5 1/2 x 8.
Nobody Listening to You? San Francisco: Philip Whalen, 1965.
>Broadside.
NOTE: Issued to celebrate "Gentle Thursday" and often listed by that title.
Highgrade: Doodles, Poems. San Francisco: Coyote's Journal, 1966.
>Wrappers.
You Didn't Even Try. San Francisco: *Coyote's Journal*, 1967.
>Wrappers.
The Invention of the Letter: A Beastly Morality {Being Illuminated Moral History for the Edification of Younger Readers}. New York: Irving Rosenthal, 1967.
>Hardcover, ring-bound.
Intransit: The Education Continues Along Including Voyages, a TransPacific Journal. Eugene, Ore.: Toad Press, 1967. 61 pp.
T/O. San Francisco: David Haselwood, 1967.
>Wrappers.
>80 copies.
On Bear's Head. New York: Harcourt, Brace & World/*Coyote's Journal*, 1969.
>Two issues, no priority:
>1. Hardcover, dust wrapper. 406 pp.
>2. Wrappers.
>"First edition."
Severance Pay. San Francisco: Four Seasons Foundation, 1970.
>Two issues, no priority:
>1. Hardcover, no priority:
>>a. Trade edition. 51 pp.
>>b. 50 copies, signed by the author. 51 pp.

2. Wrappers.
Writing 24.

Scenes of Life at the Capital. San Francisco: Maya, 1970.
Wrappers, no priority:
1. 250 copies. 74 pp.
2. 50 copies, numbered, signed by the author.
Maya Quarto Ten.
Also: Bolinas, Calif.: Grey Fox Press, 1971.
Wrappers.
"First edition."
NOTE: Expanded edition.

Imaginary Speeches for a Brazen Head. Los Angeles: Black Sparrow Press, 1972.
Two issues, no priority:
1. Hardcover, acetate dust wrapper; no priority:
   a. 200 copies, numbered, signed by the author. 156 pp.
   b. 26 copies, lettered, signed by the author.
2. Wrappers.
1,500 copies.

Looking for Help. San Francisco: Panjandrum Press, 1972.
Broadside.

In the Night. Privately published, ca. 1972.
Broadside.
100 signed copies.

On Bread & Poetry: A Panel Discussion with Gary Snyder, Lew Welch & Philip Whalen.
Berkeley, Calif.: Grey Fox Press, 1973. 48 pp.

The Kindness of Strangers: Poems 1969–1974. Bolinas, Calif.: Four Seasons Foundation,
1976. (Listed as New Departures in Four Seasons Paperback book list at back of
this edition.)
Wrappers. Writing 33. 59 pp.

Prolegomena to a Study of the Universe. Berkeley: Poltroon Press, 1976. Introduction
by Kevin Powers.
290 copies.

Zenshinji. Port Townsend: Copper Canyon Press, ca. 1977.

Prose Take. Bancroft Library, 1977.
Broadside.
Two editions.
26 lettered and signed.
50 numbered copies signed.

Anchor Steam Beer, for Michael McClure, unspeakable visions of the individual. Arthur
and Kit Knight Production, 1978.

Decompressions. Bolinas, Calif.: Grey Fox Press, 1978.
Wrappers. 86 pp.

Off the Wall, Interviews with Philip Whalen. Bolinas, Calif.: Grey Fox Press, 1978.
Wrappers.

The Diamond Noodle. Berkeley, Calif.: Poltroon Press, 1980.
Two issues:
1. 100 copies, signed and sealed by the author.
2. Wrappers.

Enough Said: Fluctuat Nec Mergitur: Poems 1974–1979. San Francisco: Grey Fox Press, 1980.

Two issues:

1. 56 hardcover copies, numbered, signed by the author. 75 pp.

2. Wrappers.

The Wind Chimes. Arif Press, 1980.

Broadside.

Tara. San Francisco: Black Stone Press, 1981.

Broadside.

100 copies.

In Takagamine, from *Scenes of Life at the Capital.* San Francisco: Black Stone Press, 1981.

Broadside.

99 copies.

Heavy Breathing. San Francisco: Grey Fox Press, 1983. 207 pp.

Wrappers.

Two Variations: All About Love. San Francisco: Arif Press, 1983. Wesley Tanner.

Broadside.

19 copies.

A Vision of the Bodhisattvas. Albuquerque, N.M.: Living Batch Bookstore, 1984. Illustration by Jeff Bryan.

Broadside.

100 copies.

For C. San Francisco: Arion Press, 1984.

First appeared in *Like I Say,* then again in *Temple of Flora.*

With illustrations by Jim Dine.

The Elizabethan Phrase. Santa Barbara, Calif.: Designed & printed by David Dahl for Table-Talk Press, 1985.

Broadside.

Two Novels. Somerville, Mass.: Zephyr Press, 1985. 250 pp.

Two editions:

1. Hardcover, dust wrapper.

    a. Trade edition. 300 copies.

    b. 50 copies signed and numbered by the author.

2. Wrappers. 1,200 copies.

Window Peak. Santa Fe, N.M.: Casa Sin Nombre, 1986. Photographs by Annie Liebowitz.

Broadside.

500 copies.

Driving Immediately Passed. Berkeley, Calif.: Poltroon Press, 1989.

First appeared in *A Bibliography of the Auerhahn Press & Its Successor Dave Haselwood Books,* compiled by a printer, Poltroon Press, 1976.

Broadside.

Canoeing Up Cabarga Creek: Buddhist Poems 1955–1986. Introduction by Richard Baker. Foreword by Allen Ginsberg. Berkeley, Calif.: Parallax Press, 1996. 68 pp.

Mark Other Place. Pacifica, Calif.: Big Bridge Press, 1997.

First appeared in Big Bridge chapbook issue January 1997.

Big Bridge Press scheduled for 1999 in two editions.
   1. 100 copies numbered.
   2. 26 copies lettered and signed by the author.
Japanese Tea Garden Golden Gate Park in Spring. Boulder, Colo.: Kavyayantra Press,
   The Naropa Institute, 1998.
   Broadside.
Some of These Days. San Jose, N.M.: Desert Rose Press, 1999.
   Two editions:
   1. 50 copies hardbound, signed by the poet.
   2. 250 copies sewn in wrappers.

ABOUT THE AUTHOR

Philip Whalen—a voice of innovation in American poetry—was born in Portland, Oregon, in October 1923. He grew up in The Dalles, a small town on the Columbia River two hours southeast of Portland. After serving with the U.S. Army Air Corps during the Second World War, he returned to the Pacific Northwest to attend Reed College, where he met fellow students Lew Welch and Gary Snyder. He eventually moved to the San Francisco Bay area, working odd jobs to support his writing. During the 1950s, he met Allen Ginsberg, Jack Kerouac, Kenneth Rexroth, and other figures in the San Francisco Renaissance. On October 6, 1955, he participated in the historical Six Gallery reading along with Kerouac, Ginsberg, Snyder, Philip Lamantia, and Michael McClure. His poetry appeared in issues of the *Evergreen Review*, as well as other small journals of the period, and in 1960 he appeared in Donald Allen's *New American Poetry* anthology. Whalen is the author of numerous books of poetry, including *Like I Say* and *Memoirs of an Interglacial Age*, which along with other early books, were published in the 1967 collection *On Bear's Head*. Since its publication, *On Bear's Head* has been a monumentally important document of the developing consciousness of his generation, and it anticipated the concerns of generations that would follow, both in exploration of style and the content possibilities. Whalen is also the author of two novels, *You Don't Even Try* and *Imaginary Speeches for a Brazen Head*. More recent poetry titles include *The Kindness of Strangers, Severance Pay, Scenes of Life at the Capital*, the collection *Heavy Breathing, Canoeing Up Cabarga Creek*, and *Some of These Days*.

Whalen's growing interest in Zen Buddhism matured during extended visits to Kyoto, Japan. In 1972 he moved to the San Francisco Zen Center, and he was ordained unsui (Zen Buddhist monk) the following year. Currently, he is retired abbot and resident teacher at the Hartford Street Zen Center in San Francisco.

PENGUIN POETS

Paul Beatty	*Joker, Joker, Deuce*
Ted Berrigan	*Selected Poems*
Philip Booth	*Pairs*
Jim Carroll	*Fear of Dreaming*
Jim Carroll	*Void of Course*
Nicholas Christopher	*5° & Other Poems*
Carl Dennis	*Ranking the Wishes*
Diane di Prima	*Loba*
Stuart Dischell	*Evenings and Avenues*
Stephen Dobyns	*Common Carnage*
Paul Durcan	*A Snail in My Prime*
Amy Gerstler	*Crown of Weeds*
Amy Gerstler	*Nerve Storm*
Debora Greger	*Desert Fathers, Uranium Daughters*
Robert Hunter	*Glass Lunch*
Robert Hunter	*Sentinel*
Barbara Jordan	*Trace Elements*
Jack Kerouac	*Book of Blues*
Ann Lauterbach	*And For Example*
Ann Lauterbach	*On a Stair*
William Logan	*Vain Empires*
Derek Mahon	*Selected Poems*
Michael McClure	*Huge Dreams: San Francisco and Beat Poems*
Michael McClure	*Three Poems*
Carol Muske	*An Octave Above Thunder*
Alice Notley	*The Descent of Alette*
Alice Notley	*Mysteries of Small Houses*
Anne Waldman	*Kill or Cure*
Rachel Wetzsteon	*Home and Away*
Philip Whalen	*Overtime: Selected Poems*
Robert Wrigley	*In the Bank of Beautiful Sins*